THE M. & E. HAND

KU-603-994

ROMAN LAW

L. B. CURZON, B.Com.
Barrister-at-Law

Omnes legum servi sumus ut liberi esse possimus
(Cicero)

MACDONALD & EVANS LTD
8 John Street, London WC1N 2HY
1966

First published November 1966
Reprinted (with corrections) May 1969
Reprinted October 1974

MACDONALD AND EVANS LTD
1966

ISBN: 0 7121 1853 5

This book is copyright and may not be
reproduced in whole *or in part* (except for
purposes of review) without the express
permission of the publishers in writing.

HANDBOOK *Conditions of Sale*

This book is sold subject to the condition
that it shall not, by way of *trade or otherwise,* be lent, resold, hired out or otherwise
circulated without the publisher's prior
consent in any form of binding or cover
other than that in which it is published
*and without a similar condition including
this condition being imposed on the subsequent purchaser.*

*Printed in Great Britain by Butler & Tanner, Ltd,
Frome and London*

GENERAL INTRODUCTION

The HANDBOOK Series of Study Notes

HANDBOOKS are a new form of printed study notes designed to help students to prepare and revise for professional and other examinations. The books are carefully programmed so as to be self-contained courses of tuition in the subjects they cover. For this purpose they comprise detailed notes, self-testing questions and hints on examination technique.

HANDBOOKS can be used on their own or in conjunction with recommended textbooks. They are written by college lecturers, examiners, and others with wide experience of students' difficulties and requirements. At all stages the main objective of the authors has been to prepare students for the practical business of passing examinations.

P. W. D. REDMOND
General Editor

NOTICE TO LECTURERS

Many lecturers are now using **HANDBOOKS** as working texts to save time otherwise wasted by students in protracted note-taking. The purpose of the series is to meet practical teaching requirements as far as possible, and lecturers are cordially invited to forward comments or criticisms to the Publishers for consideration.

AUTHOR'S PREFACE

THIS **HANDBOOK** has been designed as a study guide to the elements of Roman Private Law and is intended specifically for students preparing for first examinations in this subject. Its pattern is a series of study notes and Progress Tests.

The following plan of work is suggested for the student:

(a) *Read through the book swiftly*, omitting the Progress Tests and those sections not included in the syllabus of your particular examination. (London University, for example, does not include the Law of Wills in its Intermediate syllabus.) The object of this preliminary reading is to acquire a general view of the subject matter.

(b) *Next comes the main study of the text.* Read the chapters slowly and carefully. The study of a chapter should culminate in the Progress Test which follows at the end of the chapter. *You should not pass from one chapter to the next without having completed to your satisfaction the appropriate Progress Test.* Memorise principles, important dates and facts.

(c) *The third reading should be for revision purposes.* At this stage concentrate on the revision of broad outlines.

(d) *The fourth, and final reading* should concentrate on a revision of details of the text.

(e) *Finally, attempt, at three separate sittings*, and under examination conditions, the three *Test Papers* in Appendix III.

The student beginning his work on Roman Private Law usually asks three questions: Is a knowledge of Latin essential? Should I learn all the dates? How much of the material should I memorise?

(a) *Knowledge of Latin.* Undoubtedly this is an advantage. But unless your particular examination syllabus specifically includes the translation of passages from the Institutes, a lack of Latin should not be a handicap. In this **HANDBOOK** most of the important Latin phrases and words are followed by a translation. You are advised, however, to have a good Latin-English dictionary available for reference purposes. An occasional search of the dictionary can be valuable, since the language of Roman Law is heavy with historical overtones. The dictionary's explanation, for example, of the word *Quirites*, from which the term quiritary ownership (*see* X, 2) is derived, illumines the significance of the term in an extraordinary way.

(b) *Dates*. The most important dates must be known. The dates of the Monarchy, the Republic, the Empire, the important Emperors, must be committed to memory. Important *Senatusconsulta*, *Leges*, must also be known. Examiners expect this knowledge and often set questions which assume it (*see* for example, Appendix III, Paper 3, Question No. 3). Where only approximate dates can be given they are preceded in the text by "*c*" (as in the date attributed to the *Codex Hermogenianus—see* III, 6).

(c) *Memorisation*. The student should memorise important dates, outlines and details of important legislation, principles, rules and exceptions to those rules.

Although these study notes are self-contained, the student will wish to read more widely. The following books are recommended for the beginner.

Background reading:	*The Romans* (ed. by J. V. Balsdon, published by Watts & Co, 1965): an interesting series of essays on the historical and social background of Rome.
	Daily Life in Ancient Rome (J. Carcopino, published by Penguin Books): a vivid account of the daily life of Romans in the second century A.D.
Elements of Roman Private Law:	*An Introduction to Roman Law* (J. K. Nicholas, published by Oxford University Press, 1962): an extensive introduction to some of the problems of Roman Law.
	The Elements of Roman Law (R. W. Lee, published by Sweet and Maxwell, 1956): one of the outstanding books of its kind, containing a translation of the Institutes.
Reference:	*Textbook of Roman Law from Augustus to Justinian* (W. W. Buckland, published by Cambridge University Press,

3rd edition, 1963): a standard reference
book in this subject.

Roman Private Law (M. Kaser, published by Butterworths, 1965): a scho-
larly and detailed treatment of the principal topics of Roman Law.

Questions from past LL.B. examination papers are reprinted
by kind permission of the Senate of the University of London.

I should like to acknowledge the help I have received from
Mr L. Arridge, B.A., Librarian of the Chester College of
Further Education and from Mr P. Pocklington, F.L.A., City
Librarian of Chester.

August, 1966   L. B. C.

CONTENTS

xi

Part Four: THE LAW OF WILLS AND SUCCESSION

PART ONE

BACKGROUND AND SOURCES

CHAPTER I

HISTORICAL BACKGROUND

PERIODS IN THE HISTORY OF ROMAN LAW

1. General. Rome was founded in 753 B.C., and that part of its history which is relevant to this study of Roman Law ends with the death of Justinian in A.D. 565. It is possible to consider the history of Roman Law, in a very general manner, from a number of viewpoints:

(a) from the point of view of its general political background;
(b) from the point of view which sees its culmination in the classical period;
(c) from the point of view which considers it in relation to its constitutional background.

2. Political background. The development of Roman Law may be considered in relation to the background of general political changes in Roman society. It is possible to discern five important periods:

(a) *Prior to the XII Tables* (*see* III, **1–3**). In this period the law was based on custom and was linked with religious practices.
(b) *From the XII Tables to the subjugation of Italy* (*c.* 266 B.C.). During this era the law was rigid and was based largely on the XII Tables and their interpretation by the College of Pontiffs.
(c) *From the subjugation of Italy to the commencement of the Principate* under Augustus (27 B.C.). The outstanding accomplishments of this period were the development of the law by the Praetors (*see* **12–14** below) and the growth of *jus gentium* (*see* II, **8–9**) which embraced citizens and non-citizens.
(d) *From Augustus to Diocletian* (A.D. 284). This era included the classical period of Roman Law (*see* **3** below) and

witnessed an evolution of law based, in part, on scientific interpretation and reasoning.

(e) *From Diocletian to the conclusion of Justinian's reign* (A.D. 565). Legislation by Imperial Decree and the development of the law, together with its codification, dominated this epoch.

> NOTE: A more general interpretation of the political background of Roman Law sees its two main epochs as:
>
> (i) *The epoch of local law*—"rigid, formalistic and national," characterised by the old *jus civile* (*see* II, **10–11**), beginning with the XII Tables and continuing until the end of the Republic, and
>
> (ii) *the epoch of universal law*—"equitable and no longer highly formalistic," leading to the growth of *jus gentium* (*see* II, **8**), and continuing throughout the Empire.

3. The classical, and related periods. The development of Roman Law may be considered from another viewpoint as falling into three periods:

(a) *The pre-classical period*, prior to the Principate. In this period the most significant feature is taken to be the beginnings of legal science in the third to the first century B.C., born from the influence of Greek philosophy and methods of thought applied to Roman legal concepts.

(b) *The classical period.* This vital period may be considered to have approximated to the epoch of the Principate. In a more restricted sense it is usually held to cover the period from Hadrian (A.D. 117) to the death of Alexander Severus (A.D. 235). During this period Roman legal thought made great advances, characterised by the work of the jurists, such as Gaius, Papinian, Ulpian and Paulus.

(c) *The post-classical period* from, approximately, the third century A.D. During this period the growth of legislation by imperial decree, and the prevalence of absolutism created an atmosphere in which the advance of legal philosophy was slowed down. In the Eastern Empire under Justinian classical tendencies reasserted themselves briefly, culminating in his vast work of codification (*see* III, **11–17**).

4. General constitutional background. Yet another interpretation of the development of Roman Law sees it in relation to the three major constitutional epochs in Roman political history:

(a) The period of the Kings;
(b) The period of the Republic;
(c) The period of the Empire.

This general view is the basis of the remainder of this chapter.

THE PERIOD OF THE KINGS, 753–509 B.C.

5. The King. From its foundation, Rome was ruled by its Kings until *c.* 510 B.C. The King's powers were very extensive. He was supreme commander in time of war, and had supreme civil and criminal jurisdiction. He held the office of High Priest and his powers over his subjects included *jus vitae aut necis* (power of life or death).

6. The People. In the very early days the inhabitants of Rome were divided into three tribes: the Luceres, Tities and Ramnes. Each occupied one part of Roman territory. The tribes were divided into *curiae*, each consisting of patricians with a common name and common blood ties. By 241 B.C. there were 35 tribes. The inhabitants of Rome in the time of the Kings consisted of:

(a) *Patricians:* the nobility who were, for a long period, alone eligible to occupy the State's high offices.
(b) *Plebeians:* originally the poorer, non-privileged citizens.
(c) *Clients:* who enjoyed a status between patricians and plebeians and attached themselves to a patrician house.
(d) *Slaves:* conquered by the Roman Army and brought back in slavery to Rome.

7. The Assemblies of the People.

(a) *Comitia Curiata.* This was an assembly of patricians held in the Comitium in the centre of Rome. It consisted of about 30 curiae, each curia casting one vote according to the wishes of its majority. It was convoked by the King and his magistrates. Its duties included the choice of a King and other high officers, and the enacting of the *lex curiata de imperio*, which conferred *imperium* (full authority). With the exception of this *lex*, all its decrees needed confirmation by the Senate. Under the name of *Comitia Calata* it sanctioned wills (*see* XII, **11**), and dealt with adrogation (*see* V, **8**), meeting in March and May of each year under the Head of the College of Pontiffs (*Pontifex Maximus*).

(b) *Comitia Centuriata*. Introduced by Servius Tullus (578–535 B.C.), this assembly of the armed force of Rome became very important with the establishment of the Republic (*see* **9**(c) below).

(c) *The Senate*. The Senate acted as a consultative body to the Kings. In 580 B.C. it consisted of 300 patricians, chosen because of age and experience (*see* also **17** below).

THE PERIOD OF THE REPUBLIC, 509–27 B.C.

8. The Kings replaced. Following the expulsion of Tarquinius Superbus in 509 B.C., supreme powers were vested in two magistrates elected annually by the *Comitia Centuriata*, known first as Praetors. They were endowed with *imperium*, subject to a veto which each could exercise over the other. Increased powers were given to the Senate (*see* **9** below).

9. The Assemblies.

(a) *The Senate*. The Senators were chosen by Consuls, later by Censors. They were summoned by a magistrate (*see* note below) whom they advised on matters of peace and war. They were also required to approve decrees of the *Comitia Centuriata*. By the end of the third century B.C. the Senate had become the State's policy making executive. A *senatusconsultum* (see II, **18**) had the force of law. Sulla (81–79 B.C.) increased the number of Senators to 600. Senators held office for life, unless expelled for serious misconduct. They controlled the Treasury and nominated Dictators (high officials invested with dictatorial powers during an emergency). They were able to remove a citizen from the operation of the law, but *Lex Cornelia* (67 B.C.) enacted that at least 200 Senators were to be present when such a resolution was passed.

> NOTE: The Roman magistrate was a high state official who possessed extensive political and judicial powers. His title and office should not be confused in any way with those of the modern Justice of the Peace.

(b) *Comitia Curiata* (*see* **7**(a) above). The *Comitia* played an important role in the Republic, but lost its right of ratifying the election of magistrates.

(c) *Comitia Centuriata* (Assembly of the Centuries). Created by Servius Tullus, the *Comitia* was originally established for purposes of warfare and included patricians and plebeians. They were divided into five classes on the basis of a property qualification as assessed by the Censors. Each of the five classes provided centuries of armed men, 175 in all (later increased to 373). The wealthiest patricians also provided 18 centuries of cavalry.

The Assembly was convened by a summons of the Consuls and met in the Field of Mars. Voting took place by centuries. The functions of the Assembly came to include deciding on matters of war and the election of magistrates possessing *imperium*. From *c.* 508–287 B.C., the *Comitia* occupied a dominant position in the Roman State.

(d) *Comitia Tributa*. Established in 499 B.C., the *Comitia Tributa* was an assembly of patricians and plebeians on the basis of tribal organisation. It was convoked by a magistrate possessing *imperium*. Its enactments had the force of *leges* (laws). Initially these enactments required the *auctoritas patrum* (approbation) of the Senate, but following *Lex Publilia Philonis* (399 B.C.), this requirement became a mere formality. Its functions included the election of Quaestors (*see* **11** below). It was at the height of its powers in the third century B.C. and had disappeared by the earlier period of the Empire.

(e) *Concilium Plebis* (Meeting of the Plebeians). This assembly consisted of plebeians selected on a tribal basis. It was convoked by a Tribune, who would present suggestions for legislation, and its members enacted *plebiscita* which originally bound the plebeians only. Its functions included the election of Tribunes of the plebs and the plebeian Aediles, who assisted them. *Lex Hortensia* (287 B.C.) enacted that *plebiscita* were binding on all. The *Concilium* disappeared during the early part of the Empire.

NOTE: The process by which assemblies usually legislated commenced when a magistrate stated his proposals for legislation. These were given in the form of a request (*rogatio*). The proposals were then published by the magistrate in the form of an edict and a final vote was taken by

the assembly concerned, usually 24 days later. The voting
was oral (at a later date, by secret ballot). The assembly
could not amend the magistrate's proposed legislation, but
could only accept or reject it.

10. The XII Tables and Interpretatio. The publication of a
written code of law—The XII Tables—was the outcome of
continuing hostility between patricians and plebeians. It was
a landmark in the development of Roman Law under the
Republic and is considered in III, 1–3.

(a) *Interpretatio.* The interpretation of the XII Tables was
undertaken for one hundred years after their publication
in 450 B.C. by the College of Pontiffs, presided over by the
Pontifex Maximus. The method of *interpretatio* adopted
by the Pontiffs was an explanation of the meaning of the
Tables. This resulted in a widening of the application of
the law of the Tables and, hence, in the creation of new
law. For example, under the XII Tables, three separate
sales of a *filiusfamilias* by his father (*see* V, **8**(b)) ended
the father's power over the son. By an *interpretatio* of the
Pontiffs it was held that one sale only was needed in the
case of a grandson.

(b) *Jus Civile Flavianum.* In 304 B.C. Gnaeus Flavius published a treatise on the Civil Law, which revealed the *legis
actiones* (formulae for civil actions—*see* XXI) and the
calendar of court-days and holidays. This publication,
followed in 300 B.C. by *Lex Ogulnia*, which allowed plebeians to enter the College of Pontiffs, ended the dominant
position of the College. Sextus Aelius Paetus published,
c. 204 B.C., a *Commentaria Tripertita*, which discussed the
law as established by pontifical *interpretatio*. Publications
such as these enabled jurists outside the College to share
in the development of the civil law.

11. Magistrates and Officers of the Republic.

(a) *Consuls.* The Consuls were the highest magistrates of the
Republic. They were originally elected by the *Comitia Centuriata* (*see* **9** above). During their annual term of office
they acted as Heads of State, each having *imperium*, and
each being subject to the other's veto. They had power
to convene the Senate and to initiate legislation in the

Comitia Centuriata. The Licinio-Sextian Laws (introduced in 367 B.C. by Licinius and Sextius) enacted that one Consul had to be a plebeian. Their very extensive powers were curtailed by the growth of the Praetor's power, by the publication of the law, and by the creation of new magistracies, *e.g.* the Censors.

(b) *Praetors*. The *Leges Liciniae* established the office of Praetor Urbanus, responsible for the administration of justice. The work of the Praetors was of outstanding importance in the development of Roman Law and is considered in 12–14 below.

(c) *Censors*. Two Censors (*censere* = to assess) were first selected by the *Comitia Centuriata* in 443 B.C. in order to make assessments of property for taxation purposes. Each person enrolled on the census was registered according to his position in his tribe and *centuria*. About one hundred years later the Censors were given important powers in deciding the Senate's composition. They acted as *magistri morum* (*mos* = conduct, behaviour), in which capacity they could exclude from public office those whose behaviour had gravely offended against public morality. They had the duty of letting out the taxes to farmers of the public revenue (*publicani*) and of investing surplus revenue on behalf of the State.

(d) *Tribunes*. In 494 B.C. a meeting of plebeian legionaries decided to appoint two executive officers (Tribunes), whose persons were to be inviolable, so as to balance the power of the patrician Consuls. In the second century B.C. they obtained the right to sit in the Senate.

(e) *Quaestors*. Two Quaestors were elected annually by the *Comitia Tributa* (*see* 9(*d*) above). Their main duties involved finance and, until Augustus, they had charge of the contents of the Treasury. They possessed criminal jurisdiction in the case of political offences.

(f) *Curule Aediles*. Two Curule Aediles were first appointed by the *Comitia Tributa* in 365 B.C. The first were patricians, but, at a later date, plebeians were appointed to the office. Their functions included: *cura urbis* (care of the city, including supervision of police and buildings); *cura annonae* (care of provisions, including supervision of the markets); *cura ludorum* (organisation of public games). They had some judicial powers, including the infliction of fines in cases of grain hoarding and the use of faulty weights. The Roman Law of Sale developed as a result of their exercise of judicial powers (*see* XVII, 6(d)). *See* also XX, 8(b). The Curule Aediles issued an Edict on entering office which defined (in a similar fashion to the Praetor's Edict (*see* **13** below)) the procedure which would govern their administration.

PRAETORIAN DEVELOPMENT OF THE LAW

12. The role of the Praetors. After the expulsion of the Kings, full executive powers were vested in the Consuls. In 367 B.C. the first Praetor was appointed to carry out those duties of the Consuls which involved civil jurisdiction. In 242 B.C. a Praetor Peregrinus was appointed. The Praetor Urbanus originally had jurisdiction over Roman citizens; the Praetor Peregrinus had jurisdiction in cases involving foreigners. In addition to their judicial powers the Praetors possessed *imperium*, which included powers of military command and of summoning the Senate.

13. The Edict.

(a) The *imperium* of the Kings did not include the power to legislate; hence the *imperium* transmitted to the Consuls and Praetors did not include the power to make laws. But the power of the Praetors in administrative matters manifested itself in the issuing of important administrative regulations which, in time, came to include the provision of certain remedies at law.

(b) At the beginning of the Praetor's term of office he published his *Edictum Perpetuum* in which was set out the procedure which would govern his administration. The *Edictum Perpetuum* consisted of:

    (i) *Edictum Tralaticium* (that part of his predecessor's Edict which he intended to carry over and use), and

    (ii) *Edictum Novum* (new administrative regulations).

       NOTE: An *Edictum Repentinum* was a special administrative order published for a particular occasion.

(c) The Edict included all recognised causes of action, defences (*see* XXII, **23**), formulae for actions (*see* XXII) and other types of remedy.

(d) *Lex Cornelia de Edictis* (67 B.C.) prohibited the Praetors from varying or departing from an *Edictum Perpetuum*.

(e) The Praetor could grant an *actio in factum* in a case for which his Edict did not provide a suitable action.

14. The Edict and the Development of Law. In three important ways the Praetors, through the Edicts, developed the Roman Law:

(a) *By emendation* of the *jus civile* (*emendandi gratia*), *e.g.* the granting of *bonorum possessio* (*see* XIII, **33**) to a person who was not, in strict terms, an heir.

(b) *By supplementing* the *jus civile* (*supplendi gratia*), *e.g.* the granting of legal protection to *peregrini* (aliens or foreign residents, as opposed to Roman citizens).

(c) *By creating auxiliary remedies* (*adjuvandi gratia*), *e.g.* the granting of *actiones utiles* (*see* XXII, **6**).

NOTE

(i) The Praetor played a very important part in the creation and operation of the Formulary system (*see* XXII).

(ii) Other significant examples of Praetorian innovation can be seen in Praetorian Interdicts and the remedy of *restitutio in integrum* (*see* XXIII, **11–18**).

15. Decline of the Praetorian Edict. By the time of the Principate the Edicts were tending to remain unchanged. In A.D. 130 Salvius Julianus, a jurist (and Praetor-designate), was commissioned by Hadrian to consolidate the Edicts of the Praetors and the Curule Aediles. His work became known as the *Edictum Perpetuum* (not to be confused with the use of this term in **13**(b) above), which was later given the force of statute law. The *Edictum Perpetuum* was used in the centuries which followed as a basis for commentaries which themselves extended the equitable principles of Roman Law. The contribution of Praetorian Edicts to *jus honorarium* is discussed in II, **12**.

THE PERIOD OF THE EMPIRE, 27 B.C.–A.D. 565

16. Its foundation and development. The Republic declined, largely because it was unable to solve its administrative problems which had increased following Rome's expansion. Octavianus (known after 27 B.C. as Augustus) restored the order

which was threatening to vanish in civil war. Under the cloak
of bringing back the Republican constitution he nominally
shared power with the Senate but, in fact, ruled as a monarch.

The period from 27 B.C. is known as the Principate (*princeps*
= first citizen). From Diocletian (A.D. 284) an absolute
monarchy was in existence and that period is known as the
Dominate (*dominus* = master). The Empire was divided for
purposes of administration in A.D. 364, when Valentinian II
and Valens became joint Emperors. Rome was sacked in A.D.
410 and in A.D. 455. The Western Empire collapsed in the late
fifth century, but the Eastern Empire survived and continued,
nominally, until the fifteenth century. Justinian (*see* III, **11**)
ruled as Emperor of the East from A.D. 527–565.

17. Changes in the legal system.

(a) *The Senate. Senatusconsulta* became, after the early days
    of the Empire, a mere expression of the imperial will. The
    independence of the Senate declined and its powers withered
    away. Thus, in A.D. 282, following the murder of the
    Emperor Probus, a new Emperor, Carus, was elected by
    the military and ascended the throne without the pre-
    liminary authority of the Senate. The Emperor's power,
    based on his army, was henceforth the real source of
    legislative authority.

(b) *Imperial Decrees* (*see* II, **20**). Decrees, edicts, and various
    other pronouncements of the Emperors, known collec-
    tively as *constitutiones*, had the effect of imperial legisla-
    tion. *Orationes* (speeches) by which legislation was intro-
    duced into the Senate in the Emperor's name also acquired
    the force of law.

(c) *Consolidation of the Praetorian Edict.* Praetorian Edicts
    were consolidated at Hadrian's order (*see* **15** above). After
    this time they were no longer a source of fresh law.

(d) *Plebiscita* (*see* II, **16**). These became obsolete.

(e) *Responsa Prudentium* (*see* II, **19**). The growth in impor-
    tance of the jurists' opinions was of great significance. See
    also the Law of Citations (II, **19**(d)).

(f) *Powers of the Magistrates.* The powers of Praetors and
    Quaestors declined with the growth in the powers of the
    Emperors and their officials. Consuls were appointed by
    the Emperor; occasionally the office of Consul was held by

the Emperor himself. Justinian abolished the office of Consul in A.D. 541.

(g) *Replacement of the Formulary System* (*see* XXII). Under Diocletian, the Formulary System began to be replaced by the *cognitio extraordinaria* (*see* XXIII). The Emperors Constans and Constantinius completed its replacement.

(h) *Codification.* The vast programme of consolidation and codification undertaken by Justinian is discussed in III, 11–17.

PROGRESS TEST 1

1. What is meant by "the classical period" of Roman Law? (**3**)

2. Give a short account of (a) the *Comitia Centuriata*, (b) the *Comitia Tributa*. (**7, 9**)

3. What were the functions of (a) the Consuls, (b) the Curule Aediles? (**11**)

4. What was *Jus Civile Flavianum*? Account for its importance. (**10**)

5. Explain (a) *Edictum tralaticium*, (b) *Edictum novum*. (**13**)

6. In what ways did the Praetors affect the development of Roman Law? (**14**)

7. What changes in legislative forms took place under the Empire? (**17**)

8. What were the functions of (a) the Quaestors, (b) the Censors? (**11**)

9. Explain the importance of (a) *Interpretatio*, (b) *Concilium Plebis*. (**9, 10**)

CHAPTER II

THE CONCEPT OF JUS AND THE SOURCES OF ROMAN LAW

JUS

1. Its meaning. The word *jus* had a variety of meanings in Roman Law. It could refer, for example, to "a place where justice is dispensed" (*e.g. in jus vocatio*—*see* XXI, **5**), or "strict law" as distinct from equity (*see* **2** below), or "a right deriving from a rule" (*e.g. jus conubii*, the right to contract a marriage under the civil law—*see* VI), or "general man-made law as opposed to *fas*, *i.e.* law declared by divine authority". It came to have two particularly important meanings:

(a) *The rules of law;*
(b) *The rights conferred by those rules on a person in a particular situation.*

2. Jus and Aequitas. In the classical period (*see* I, **3**) **aequitas** (= fairness, justice) was the term often used in reference to the Praetorian interpretation and application of the law (*see* I, **12–14**).

3. The Precepts of law (jus). These are enumerated in the Institutes (*see* III, **15**) as "to live honourably, not to hurt one another, to give each man his due." Justice is defined as "the constant and perpetual wish to give each man his due."

JUS PUBLICUM AND JUS PRIVATUM

4. Jus Publicum. Public Law is explained in the Institutes as "that which looks to the standing of the affairs of Rome." It was that part of the Roman Law which was concerned with the relation of the individual to the State and included:

(a) criminal law;
(b) constitutional law;

(c) ecclesiastical law;
(d) administrative law.

5. Jus Privatum. Private Law is explained in the Institutes as "that which looks to the advantage of individuals." It was that part of the Roman Law which was concerned with the relationship of individuals to one another and included:

(a) the law of family relationships;
(b) the law of obligations;
(c) the law of succession;
(d) the law of property.

> NOTE: The Institutes (*see* III, **15**) are concerned almost exclusively with Private Law.

6. The Origins of Private Law. The Institutes speak of Private Law as being threefold (*jus tripertitum*) and made up from the precepts of *jus naturale*, *jus gentium* and *jus civile* (considered below).

JUS NATURALE

7. Its meaning. "*Jus naturale* is what nature has taught all living things." (The Institutes.) This was essentially a philosophical concept. As applied to the law it suggested that there were rules of universal application derived from the common nature of all peoples and that these rules ought to be observed by all mankind. Paul, the jurist, speaks, for example, of leases as "suggested by nature itself and to be found in the law of all nations." *Jus naturale* came to be considered as an ideal to which the law should seek to conform.

JUS GENTIUM

8. Its meaning. The term *jus gentium* (= law of peoples) had two important meanings:

(a) that law which, being of *universal application* (as was *jus naturale*) was in general use among civilised peoples;
(b) that part of Roman Law which was originally applicable to *relationships between Roman citizens and foreigners* living within its jurisdiction and which was used subsequently to govern the relationships of citizens *inter se*.

9. Its development and characteristics. *Jus gentium* probably originated in the rules and administrative procedures formulated and used by the Praetor Peregrinus (*see* I, **12**) in the regulation of commercial transactions between Roman citizens and non-citizens. From its beginnings as a type of Law Merchant it developed into a general body of substantive law possessing the important characteristics of convenience and universality. A significant and vital development was the creation of a system of procedure involving the use of formulae (*see* XXII) which was less rigid and more convenient than the very formal system of *legis actiones* (*see* XXI). *Lex Aebutia* (*c.* 120 B.C.) allowed the Praetor Urbanus to use this system in cases governed by *jus civile* (*see* **10** below). Hence principles of *jus gentium* were introduced directly into the system of jurisdiction for which the Praetor Urbanus was responsible. At a later date the term *jus gentium* shed its meaning of a body of law confined to commercial transactions; its scope was widened so as to take in rules of general application, and the meaning of the term developed into that given at **8**(b) above. It eventually superseded *jus civile* (*see* below).

Of *jus gentium* Vinogradoff writes, "It arose by the side of the national *jus civile* as a body of rules suggested by fairness, common sense, knowledge of the world and some acquaintance with foreign law. The magistrates who were entrusted with jurisdiction in these cases based their decisions and the prospective rules of their Edicts on general considerations of equity and utility (*ex bono et aequo*)."

JUS CIVILE

10. Its meaning. "The law each people has settled for itself is peculiar to the State itself, and is called *jus civile* as being peculiar to that very State." (The Institutes.) The term came to be used in a number of ways:

(a) as indicating the law of a *particular state*;
(b) as referring to the *law of Rome*;
(c) as referring to that *part of Roman Law available only to citizens, e.g.* quiritary ownership (*see* X, **2**).
(d) as indicating a *comparison* with *jus gentium* (*see* **8** above) or *jus militare* (the law as applied to soldiers) or *jus honorarium* (*see* **12** below);

(e) as referring to that part of Roman Law based on *ancient customs and statutes*, particularly the XII Tables (*see* III, 1–3);

(f) as referring to the *entire corpus of Roman Law*.

The meaning of the phrase depends on its context.

11. Its features. The ancient *jus civile* was characterised by rigidity, an excessive formalism and principles rooted in an agricultural community based on family and clan organisation. As Rome expanded, as commercial contacts with foreigners increased, the simplicities and formalities of *jus civile* proved unsuited to new conditions and it was superseded in time by *jus gentium*, in which formalities played a relatively unimportant role.

JUS HONORARIUM

12. Its meaning. *Jus honorarium* referred to the body of law issuing from the Edicts of the Magistrates, in particular those of the Praetors (*see* I, **13**) and Curule Aediles (*see* I, **11**). The Edicts of the Praetors enabled them to introduce and enforce legal principles and forms which had no basis in statute. Praetorian interdicts (*see* XXIII, **11–16**), the *exceptio* (*see* XXII, **23**), *restitutio in integrum* (*see* XXIII, **17**) were examples of the renovation and extension which formed the particular contribution of *jus honorarium* to Roman Law (*see* also I, **12–14**).

JUS NON SCRIPTUM AND JUS SCRIPTUM

13. Their meaning. *Jus scriptum* (written law) included that part of the law which was put into written form on being enacted. At the time of Justinian the *jus scriptum* comprised *leges* (**15** below), *plebiscita* (**16** below), *edicta magistratuum* (**17** below), *senatusconsulta* (**18** below), *responsa prudentium* (**19** below), *constitutiones principum* (**20** below). *Jus non scriptum* (unwritten law) was considered to be that which had arisen out of custom or usage.

SOURCES OF ROMAN LAW

14. General. The sources discussed below are those which comprised the *jus scriptum* in Justinian's time (*see* **13** above).

15. Leges. Those laws resulting from the deliberations of the Roman people in their assemblies (*see* I) on the proposals of magistrates were known as *leges*. *Leges Regiae* (enactments of the Kings) were laws supposedly enacted by the early Kings of Rome. The foundation of Roman Law was considered by the Romans to be the *lex* embodied in the XII Tables (*see* III, **1–3**).

16. Plebiscita. An enactment of the *Concilium Plebis* (*see* I, **9**) was known as a *plebiscitum*. *Plebiscita* in their original form were binding only on the plebeians, but *Lex Hortensia* (287 B.C.) extended their application so that they had full statutory force.

17. Edicta Magistratuum (Edicts of the Magistrates). Rules published by those magistrates who possessed *jus edicendi* (the power of issuing edicts), *e.g.* the Praetors and Curule Aediles (*see* I, **11**), were known as Edicts. From this important source flowed the vital stream of *jus honorarium* (*see* **12** above) which swept away much of the rigidity of early Roman Law and introduced more flexible rules and forms of procedure.

18. Senatusconsulta (Resolutions of the Senate). Under the Republic a *senatusconsultum* was a direction to a magistrate. It took legal effect only when it became part of a magistrate's edict. Under the Empire, resolutions of the Senate lost their importance; the Senate acted merely to confirm proposals of the Emperors. By the end of the third century A.D. *senatusconsulta* had given way to *Constitutiones Principum* (*see* **20** below).

19. Responsa Prudentium (Replies of the Jurists).

(a) *In early Rome* the knowledge and interpretation of the law was the monopoly of the *College of Pontiffs*. The publication by Gnaeus Flavius in 304 B.C. of the formulae of *legis actiones* and the calendar of court-days ended this monopoly (*see* I, **10**). In 254 B.C. the first plebeian Pontifex Maximus, Tiberius Coruncanius, made a public declaration of his willingness to give information on matters of the law to those who applied for it. The work of Sextus Aelius Paetus (*see* I, **10**) also helped to bring the function of interpreting the law into the hands of laymen.

18551171

(b) *There arose a group of professional jurists (jurisprudentes)* who concerned themselves with considering and interpreting the XII Tables and the Edicts of the Praetors. Their importance grew and in time they engaged in drafting of documents (*scribere*), giving advice on procedure (*cavere*), giving advice in actions to advocates on behalf of litigants (*agere*) and giving opinions on legal matters generally (*respondere*).

> NOTE: A jurist did not represent a litigant in court; this was the task of an advocate (*see also* XXII, **17,** note (*v*)).

(c) *Under Augustus jus respondendi* (the right of replying to questions of law) was granted to distinguished jurists. Their opinions, sealed (*signata*) and given with the authority of Augustus, were binding on a judge. Under Hadrian, where *responsa* conflicted, a judge could prefer the one he considered most suitable.

(d) *Jus Respondendi died out* by the end of the third century A.D. The collected writings of eminent jurists of the past came to be treated as authoritative statements of the law. In A.D. 426, the Valentinian Law of Citations attempted to deal with problems arising from the mass of *responsa*.

The Law stated that:

(i) the writings of the great jurists (Papinian, Gaius, Paul, Modestinus, Ulpian) were confirmed, and

(ii) where there was a conflict of jurists' opinions, the judge must follow the majority opinion; where opinions were equal, Papinian's opinion was to prevail; where opinions were equal and Papinian had expressed no opinion, the judge was free to adopt any opinion.

(e) *Responsa contributed in large measure* to the development of Roman Law. Important examples were: the recognition of *fideicommissa* (*see* XIII, **32**) as having legal effect, the recognition of the principles of innominate contracts (*see* XVIII), and the recognition of *codicilli* as being legally binding (*see* XIII, **30**).

> NOTE: Two important and rival schools of jurists grew up in the early Empire: the Sabinians (named after Massurius Sabinus, who had received the *jus respondendi* from Tiberius) led by Ateius Capito, an eminent jurist of Augustus's period, and the Proculians (named after Proculus) led by Antistius Labeo. Their doctrinal differences are not known

A/349.37

precisely. It has been suggested that the Sabinians favoured the doctrines of *jus gentium*, while the Proculians preferred the *jus civile*. Examples of their differences in opinion may be seen in VII, **1** and X, **7**.

20. Constitutiones Principum (Imperial Constitutions). In the later stages of the Empire unrestricted legislative power passed into the hands of the Emperors. They legislated in four important modes which were known collectively as *constitutiones:*

(a) *Edicta:* By issuing proclamations in the capacity of chief magistrate.
(b) *Mandata:* By issuing binding instructions to subordinate officials e.g. governors of provinces.
(c) *Decreta:* By judicial decisions given, for example, on appeal (*see* XXIII, **20**).
(d) *Rescripta:* By giving written answers to those who had consulted the Emperor on a point of law. The queries of an inferior magistrate were answered by *epistolae*, the queries of private citizens were answered by *subscriptiones*.
(e) *Orationes:* By submission, in the earlier Empire, of a bill to the Senate.

PROGRESS TEST 2

1. What did the Romans understand by *jus*? **1(1–3)**
2. What was meant by *jus publicum*? (**4**)
3. Explain the meaning and significance of *jus naturale*. (**7**)
4. Give an account of the development of *jus gentium*. (**9**)
5. What were the meanings attached to the phrase *jus civile*? (**10**)
6. Outline the main features of *jus honorarium*. (**12**)
7. Explain (a) *plebiscita*, (b) *senatusconsulta*. (**16, 18**)
8. Account for the importance in Roman Law of *responsa prudentium*. (**19**)
9. Outline the main features of the Valentinian Law of Citations. (**19**)
10. Explain the content and importance of *constitutiones principum*. (**20**)

CHAPTER III

THE CODIFICATION OF ROMAN LAW

THE TWELVE TABLES

1. Their origin.

(a) *One of the main reasons for the political strife between patricians and plebeians* during the early years of the Republic was the dissatisfaction of the plebeians with the law and its administration. The law was uncertain and knowledge of it was not available to the plebeians. Judgments were often given on the basis of customs which were unwritten and preserved by a small group of patrician scholars. Plebeian customs relied for their enforcement on magistrates who were patricians, and the administration of the law by Consuls drawn from the patrician class was often harsh and tended to favour patrician interests, particularly in the matter of the occupation of public lands.

(b) *The Tribune Gaius Terentilius Arsa suggested* in 462 B.C. that the powers of the Consuls should be defined by a committee of five. The plebeians supported this measure but the Senate would not give its support. In 452 B.C. three representatives visited Greece and the Greek settlements in Sicily and Lower Italy to investigate Solon's Code of Laws. After their return to Rome, a group of ten patricians (the Decemvirs) was appointed and compiled ten tables of laws which were later given approval by the Senate and the *Comitia Centuriata* (*see* I, **7**).

(c) *In 450 B.C. another commission*, including plebeian members, was appointed and produced a further two tables. These, together with the ten produced by the Decemvirs were known as the XII Tables (*Lex XII Tabularum*). They were inscribed, on bronze tablets, or on wood faced with stucco, and were posted in the Forum. It is assumed that the tablets were destroyed in the sack of Rome by the Gauls (390 B.C.).

2. Their content.

(a) *The contents of the Tables* are not available in their entirety and our knowledge of them is culled from references in legal literature and the writings of Cicero and others. The Tables did not form a complete code in our sense of that phrase, since, for example, some aspects of private law were not dealt with. The laws in the surviving text are peremptory in tone; often very harsh ("False witnesses are to be hurled from the Tarpeian rock"; "Deformed children may be destroyed immediately by the father"), often seemingly trivial ("Slaves' bodies may not be embalmed"; "Not more than ten flute-players may be hired for a funeral"), but often, given their historical context, of great significance ("No law shall be passed which affects an individual only: all laws must have general application"; "No one may put another to death except after formal trial and sentence").

(b) It would seem that *the Tables included no new law*, but declared the existing customary law which had been a major cause of patrician-plebeian disputes. It is believed that the Tables were set out as follows:

> Tables I, II, III—*Civil procedure and execution*
> Table IV—*Patria Potestas*
> Tables V, VI, VII—*Guardianship, inheritance, property*
> Table VIII—*Crimes*
> Table IX—*Public law*
> Table X—*Sacred law*
> Tables XI, XII—*Supplementary laws*

3. Their importance

(a) *Romans venerated them* as the origin of their legal history.

(b) They represented an important step in the *replacement of customary law by written law*.

(c) *They were known to large numbers of persons* as a result of being displayed publicly.

(d) *They symbolised an advance* in the struggle to secure equality before the law for plebeians and patricians.

(e) *They were not entirely superseded* for about a thousand years.

OTHER CODIFICATION PRIOR TO JUSTINIAN

4. Edictum Perpetuum of Salvius Julianus. A revision and arrangement of the Edicts of the Praetors and Curule Aediles was undertaken in A.D. 130 by Salvius Julianus acting on a commission from Hadrian (*see* I, **15**).

5. Codex Gregorianus. At the end of the third century A.D. a collection of Imperial Constitutions (*see* II, **20**) from Hadrian to the end of the third century A.D. was made by Gregorianus, probably at the command of Diocletian. It consisted of sixteen books, each divided into titles, containing *rescripta* (*see* II, **20**(d)) of Septimius Severus and his successors.

6. Codex Hermogenianus. A supplement to the *Codex Gregorianus* was issued *c.* A.D. 365. It consisted of *constitutiones* of Diocletian and Maximian.

7. Codex Theodosianus. In A.D. 435 the Emperor Theodosius formed a sixteen-man commission, under the jurist Antiochus, to prepare a vast collection of *constitutiones* from the time of Constantine. The commission's work was published in A.D. **438** at Constantinople and, in the Western Empire, by Valentinian III. The code consists of sixteen books, each subdivided into titles in which the *constitutiones* are arranged chronologically. Private Law occupies the first five books and is followed by Public Law, Civil and Criminal Law, Municipal, Military and Ecclesiastical Law.

8. Edictum Theodorici. Three codifications of law were made *c.* A.D. 500 after the Western Empire had been conquered by the barbarians. The first of these *Leges Barbarorum* was compiled at the command of Theodoric, King of the Ostrogoths. It consisted of 154 sections devoted to Public and Private Law and was drawn from the works of the jurists (particularly Paulus) and the *Codex Gregorianus, Hermogenianus and Theodosianus*.

9. Breviarium Alaricianum (The Breviary of Alaric), or Lex Romana Visigothorum. In A.D. 506 a commission appointed by Alaric II, King of the Western Goths, published a *breviarium* (= epitome) made up of selections from the Theodosian Code, the Institutes of Gaius (*see* **15** below), and the writings of Paul and Papinian.

10. Lex Romana Burgundionum (Law of the Burgundians). Published *c.* A.D. 517 by King Gundobald, or his son Sigismund, this code consisted of 47 titles based on the Breviary of Alaric.

JUSTINIAN'S CODIFICATION OF THE LAW

11. Justinian and the Corpus Juris Civilis. Flavius Anicius Justinianus, born in what is now Serbia, of Slav parents, came to the throne in A.D. 527. At that date the law of the Empire consisted of: *jus vetus* (the old law), which included those *leges* of the Republic and early Empire which had not fallen into disuse, *senatusconsulta*, and a large number of juristic writings of former epochs, and *jus novum* (the new law), which consisted of numerous Imperial Constitutions (*see* II, **20**). Justinian immediately commenced an extensive process of legal reform which culminated in the massive *Corpus Juris Civilis*, consisting of:

(a) *Codex Vetus* (*see* **12** below).
(b) *Digesta, or Pandectae* (*see* **13** below).
(c) *Quinquaginta Decisiones* (*see* **14** below).
(d) *Institutiones* (*see* **15** below).
(e) *Codex Repetitae Praelectionis* (*see* **16** below).
(f) *Novellae Constitutiones* (*see* **17** below).

12. Codex Vetus (The Old Code) A.D. **529.** A commission of ten ministers of state, two leading advocates and Theophilus, a professor at Constantinople, was appointed to consolidate the Imperial Constitutions by scrapping those which had fallen into disuse and those which were considered to be irrelevant. Those constitutions of relevance were to be summarised. The work (*Justinianeus Codex*, or *Codex Vetus*) was completed in just over one year and was ratified in A.D. 529. The *Codex* consisted of 12 books.

13. Digesta, or Pandectae, A.D. **533.**

(a) *In A.D. 530 Justinian appointed Tribonian*, an eminent jurist (who had been a member of the commission responsible for the *Codex Vetus*) to head a commission of sixteen, made up of professors of the law and members of the bar. Their task was to study the writings of the great jurists who had been given *jus respondendi* (*see* II, **19**(c)). They were to extract from the writings that which was valuable and they were to scrap any repetition or contradictions. They were allowed to adapt the jurists' language so that it was relevant to the law of Justinian's time. The result of their work was to be published in 50 books, arranged in titles.

(b) *The work, for which ten years had been allowed*, was completed in three years. The writings of 39 jurists, totalling three million lines, were reduced to 150,000 lines, consisting of 9,123 extracts. The arrangement followed the general order of the *Edictum Perpetuum* of Julianus (*see* I, **15**) and may have reflected the work of three separate sub-committees which examined in particular:

   (i) Ulpian's commentaries on Sabinus and associated writers;
   (ii) Writings on the Edict;
   (iii) The works of Papinian and associated writers.

(c) *The Digest was published in December, A.D. 533*. Commentaries on it were forbidden.

14. Quinquaginta Decisiones, A.D. 529–532. Prior to the commencement of work on the Digest, and during its compilation, a number of problems of interpretation arose. By enacting a series of *constitutiones*, Justinian settled these controversies. The enactments became known as "The Fifty Decisions".

15. Institutiones (The Institutes), A.D. 533. Tribonian, Dorotheus (professor of law at Beirut) and Theophilus were entrusted with the compilation of a legal textbook for students, to be based on the Institutes of Gaius (see Note below). The compilers were instructed to eliminate from Gaius that which was obsolete and to do whatever was necessary to produce a useful, elementary treatise on the law. The Institutes, divided into four books, were published in November, A.D. 533 and their arrangement follows that used by Gaius in his Institutes.

NOTE: Gaius (his full name is unknown) lived between A.D. 130–180. He may have been a professor of law at Troas, in Asia. His writings included the Institutes, a commentary on the XII Tables and a treatise on the Edicts of the Magistrates. He may have belonged to the Sabinian school (*see* II, **19**), and was one of the five jurists whose writings were recognised as authoritative by the Law of Citations (*see* II, **19**(d)). The Digest (*see* **13** above) contains 535 extracts from his works.

16. Codex Repetitae Praelectionis, A.D. **534**. A commission of four (Dorotheus and three advocates) was appointed, under the supervision of Tribonian, to incorporate the *Quinquaginta Decisiones* (*see* **14** above) with a new edition of the *Codex Vetus* (*see* **12** above). The revised *Codex* was promulgated in A.D. 534; its preface was a constitution (*Cordi Nobis*) which gave it authority. It consists of 12 books of 4,652 *constitutiones* dating from the time of Hadrian.

17. Novellae Constitutiones post Codicem (Enactments, or Novels, subsequent to the publication of the Code). About 165 *constitutiones* enacted after the *Codex Repetitae Praelectionis*, between A.D. 534–565, are preserved. Most relate to ecclesiastical and public matters; some deal with important reforms in the law of intestate succession.

PROGRESS TEST 3

1. Give an account of the political background to the introduction of the XII Tables. **(1)**

2. Outline the general contents of the XII Tables. **(2)**

3. Account for the importance in Roman legal history of the XII Tables. **(1–3)**

4. What were (a) *Codex Gregorianus*, (b) *Codex Theodosianus*? **(5, 7)**

5. Give an account of (a) *Edictum Theodorici*, (b) Alaric's Breviary. **(8, 9)**

6. Explain (a) *Quinquaginta Decisiones*, (b) The Novels. **(14, 17)**

7. Outline the general contents of the Digest. What was its importance in Roman legal history? **(13)**

8. What was the relation of the Institutes of Justinian to the Institutes of Gaius? What is known of Gaius? **(15)**

9. What was the *Codex Repetitae Praelectionis*? **(16)**

10. "His main achievement in law was to consolidate rather than to innovate." Discuss this estimate of Justinian's work. **(11–17)**

11. "The most celebrated system of jurisprudence known to the world begins, as it ends, with a Code." (Maine). Discuss. **(1–17)**

PART TWO

THE LAW OF PERSONS

CHAPTER IV

CLASSIFICATION OF PERSONS AND CAPITIS DEMINUTIO

THE LAW OF PERSONS

1. General. The law of Persons was concerned with the different types of status and legal rights enjoyed by persons. "The main distinction in the law of Persons," says Gaius (*see* III, **15**), "is that all men are either free or slaves." Rights depended on one's status; hence the rights enjoyed by a slave, or a son in power, for example, differed substantially from those enjoyed by a *paterfamilias* (*see* V).

CLASSIFICATION OF PERSONS

2. Classfication used in the Institutes. Persons were classified according to the following categories:

(a) Free or Unfree;
(b) *Sui Juris* or *Alieni Juris*;
(c) Under Guardianship or Not Under Guardianship.

3. The First Division of Persons. Persons might be free or unfree. Those who were not free were either in slavery (*see* VIII) or in quasi-servile conditions *e.g. mancipium* (civil bondage) (*see* VIII, **13**).

4. The Second Division of Persons. Persons might be *sui juris* (of independent status) or *alieni juris* (in the power of others). Thus, sons in the power of their fathers (*see* V) were said to be *alieni juris*. Slaves in the power of their masters (*see* VIII) were also *alien juris*. A *paterfamilias* (see V) was *sui juris*.

5. The Third Division of Persons. Persons who were *sui juris* might have a guardian, or not. Two kinds of guardianship existed:

(a) *Tutela* (*see* VII, **5**);
(b) *Cura* (*see* VII, **13**).

CAPITIS DEMINUTIO

6. Its meaning. When a person underwent a change in his status, he was said to have suffered *capitis deminutio* (deterioration of status). The status of a freeman reflected his rights, considered under three heads (*tria capita*):

(a) *Status Familiae*—Family rights;
(b) *Status Libertatis*—Freedom;
(c) *Status Civitatis*—Citizenship.

7. The three types of Capitis Deminutio.

(a) *Capitis Deminutio Minima* (the least diminution). The family rights of a person were changed, but he retained freedom and citizenship, as, for example, where a person *alieni juris* becomes *sui juris* by emancipation (see example below), or where one who is *sui juris* is adopted (*see* V, **8**). In these cases status could not be said to have deteriorated; rather, one had changed families.

> EXAMPLE: Marcus, son of Brutus, and in his *potestas*, is emancipated by Brutus (*see* V, **12**). As a result, Marcus is said to have undergone *capitis deminutio*.

(b) *Capitis Deminutio Minor vel Media* (the less diminution). This change involved a loss of citizenship, but freedom was retained, *e.g.* by suffering banishment or deportation.
(c) *Capitis Deminutio Maxima* (the greater diminution). In this case all rights were lost as, for example, when a freeman was made a slave.

8. The effects of Capitis Deminutio.

(a) *C.D. Minima.* A person lost those rights he had enjoyed through membership of the family to which he had belonged.

EXAMPLE: Flavius, son of Cinna, leaves his natural family and enters the family of Marullus (*see* V). In so doing he loses the right, which he enjoyed as a member of Cinna's family, of succeeding his father on intestacy.

(b) *C.D. Minor.* The rights of a citizen in civil and general political affairs were lost.

EXAMPLE: Cominius suffers *capitis deminutio minor*. As a result he loses the right to vote (*jus suffragii*), the right to acquire property (*commercium*), the right to hold an office (*jus honorum*) and the right to become a partner in a legal marriage (*conubium*). If Cominius were married according to the civil law, the marriage would be considered as having ended (although the union might be maintained as *matrimonium jure gentium*—marriage under the *jure gentium*).

(c) *C.D. Maxima.* This took from a person all those rights enjoyed by a free Roman citizen.

NOTE

(i) Where a man changes only his social standing, as, for example, by ceasing to hold a public office, he does not suffer *capitis deminutio* as a result.

(ii) The manumission of a slave (*see* VIII, **9**) does not involve *capitis deminutio*, since a slave does not possess *caput* (*i.e.* political and social rights).

PROGRESS TEST 4

1. "Persons might be free or unfree." Discuss. (**1–5**)
2. What was meant by the following terms: (a) *sui juris*, (b) *alieni juris*, (c) *status familiae*? (**4, 6**)
3. Explain the meaning of *capitis deminutio*. (**6**)
4. What is the difference between *capitis deminutio minima* and *capitis deminutio maxima*? (**7**)
5. What were the effects of *capitis deminutio minor*? (**8**)

CHAPTER V

PATRIA POTESTAS

ITS MEANING AND SIGNIFICANCE

1. Definition. *Patria Potestas* (paternal power) meant the power exercised by the head of a family (*paterfamilias*) over the members of that family. They and their property, with some few exceptions, were subjected to this power until it was ended by the death of the *paterfamilias* or by some other special circumstances (*see* **12** and **13** below). Only the Roman citizen had the right to wield this power; to lose one's citizenship was to lose one's *potestas* over a family.

2. The Roman Family.

(a) *Under Roman Law, the basis of the family* was the absolute power of the *paterfamilias*. He was the representative of the family, *e.g.* he alone possessed the right of suing upon a contract made with a member of the family. The family was organised as a monocracy—a close community under the rule of one person—and has been described as "living under one roof, with one purse, one altar and one worship."

(b) *The familia was based on agnatic relationship* derived from the authority of the *paterfamilias*. It consisted of *agnates*, *i.e.* (i) blood relations traced solely through males, excluding all those males and females who had left the family, and (ii) those who had come into the family, *e.g.* by adoption. The term *cognates* referred to blood relations only, whether agnates or not. As the law developed cognation became of more importance than agnation.

(c) *The power exercised by the paterfamilias* was, in early times, absolute and included the right to inflict capital punishment (*see* **3** below). It continued even after the children had reached their majority; thus the consent of the *paterfamilias* was needed by a son (*filiusfamilias*) who wished to marry, no matter what his age.

(d) *Because of the importance attached to the preservation and perpetuation of the family and its name*, the institution of adoption (*see* **8** below) was of great importance.

3. Patria Potestas as it affected members of the family.

(a) In early times the *paterfamilias* had the power of life and death (*jus vitae necisque*) over his children. This extreme power disappeared gradually. The Censor (*see* I, **11**) was able to punish a *paterfamilias* who had abused his power. An author of Hadrian's time makes the plea, "*Patria Potestas in pietate debet, non atrocitate consistere.*" ("Paternal power must consist of love and not of cruelty.") *Jus vitae necisque* was abolished by Constantine, under whom a father who had killed his son suffered the dreadful death also meted out to a parricide.

(b) *The power of noxal surrender* (*see* **XX**, **6**) belonged at one time to the *paterfamilias*, who was liable for a delict committed by those in his power. A noxal action allowed him the alternative of surrendering the wrongdoer or paying damages. The power of noxal surrender of sons was abolished by Justinian.

(c) *Those in potestas had no proprietary rights*, hence, that which they acquired belonged, in general, to the *paterfamilias* (*see* **4** below). *See* also XVII, 25(c).

(d) *Although children in potestas were considered to be free*, the *paterfamilias* alone had the right to give them in adoption and marriage, to emancipate (*see* **12** below) and, under the early law, to control divorce.

(e) *The power of selling children into slavery* could be exercised in early times by the *paterfamilias*, but was virtually obsolete in the time of Justinian. The sale of children had been forbidden by Diocletian, and this prohibition was continued under Constantine who made an exception in the case of very poor parents, to whom he gave the right to sell a newly-born child. This exception, with the right of redemption, continued under Justinian, but he prohibited a creditor's receiving a child in pledge.

4. Patria Potestas as it affected the property of the family.
Because children in *potestas* lacked proprietary rights, the family's property was owned absolutely by the *paterfamilias*

and administered by him for the common benefit of the family.
This absolute ownership was modified by the creation of rights
to *peculium* (*i.e.* property a son might hold independently).

(a) *Peculium Profecticium.* This included property given to
the son in contemplation of a benefit to be received by the
father, and gifts made to the son by his father.

(b) *Peculium Castrense.* (*Castrensis* = pertaining to a camp).
Augustus allowed a son to keep that which he had obtained
on military service, *e.g.* gifts for military equipment, pay,
property captured from the enemy. Property so acquired
could be disposed of by the son's will and was available in
satisfaction of contracts into which he had entered or
delicts he had committed. Before Justinian, this property
reverted to the father on the son's intestacy. Justinian
gave the children and brothers and sisters of the son a right
of succession on intestacy.

(c) *Peculium Quasi-Castrense.* Constantine extended the privileges of *peculium* to property acquired by certain officials
in *patria potestas*, *e.g.* officials of the Imperial Palace,
keepers of records, advocates of the Praetorian Court,
bishops, deacons and presbyters. Justinian allowed the disposition by will of this property.

(d) *Bona Materna.* Constantine allowed a son to inherit *bona
materna* (property left by the mother). The son owned the
property subject to a *usufruct* (*see* XI, **9**) held by the *paterfamilias*. In such a case the *paterfamilias* had the duty of
diligently administering the property; he could not alienate
the property in any way and, on his death, his interest
passed directly to the son.

(e) *Bona Adventicia.* In A.D. 395 *bona materna* was extended
so as to include any property coming to the son from a
maternal ancestor beyond the mother, including gifts *inter
vivos* or acquisitions by will. Such property was known as
bona adventicia. Where a son was emancipated by his
father (*see* **12** below), Justinian allowed the father to retain
a usufruct in one-half of the *bona adventicia*.

ITS CREATION

5. By legitimate birth. Where a father and child were subject to the *jus civile* (*see* II, **10**) and the child had been conceived in lawful wedlock, *potestas* was created at birth.

NOTE
  (i) Both parents had to be Roman citizens, or
 (ii) The father had to be a Roman citizen and possess *conubium* (see VI, **9**) and
(iii) The marriage had to be valid under *jus civile*.

6. By marriage. The marriage had to be under the civil law. As a result of *manus* marriage (*see* VI, **14**) the wife passed into the power of her husband's *paterfamilias*. In free marriage (*see* VI, **15**) the wife remained under the *potestas* of the head of her own family.

7. By legitimation (*see* VI, **29**). One of the results of legitimation was that natural children, now legitimated, came under the power of their father.

8. By adoption. In order to prevent a family becoming extinct, Roman law allowed a person to be admitted into the family of another, as a result of which he was subjected, in certain circumstances, to the *potestas* of the new *paterfamilias*.

There were two types of adoption: *adrogatio* (where the person adopted was *sui juris*) and *adoptio* (where the person adopted was *alieni juris*).

(a) *Adrogatio*

   (i) *Before Justinian.* The mode of adrogation was public in character, requiring a preliminary investigation by the Pontifex Maximus and the agreement of the *Comitia Calata* (*see* I, **7**), or later, of the thirty Lictors who represented the *curiae* in the *Comitia Calata*. Their consent was not given unless the *adrogatus* (*i.e.* the person being adrogated) had a brother who could continue the family worship. Under early law, *impubes* (boys under 14, girls under 12) could not be adrogated. Antoninus Pius removed this prohibition subject to: a preliminary enquiry; the *adrogator* giving security for the restoration of the property of the *adrogatus* to his family on his death; a promise by the *adrogator* not to emancipate the *adrogatus* except for a good reason; the right of the *adrogatus*, if emancipated without just cause, or disinherited, to the restoration of his property, plus one-fourth of the adrogator's estate on the latter's death (the *Quarta Antonina*). *Under Justinian.* Imperial Rescript became the usual method of effecting adrogation. It was necessary to

(iii) establish that the *adrogatus* had consented, and that the *adrogator* had no adopted or natural children, was over 60, and at least 18 years older than the *adrogatus*.

(iii) *Effects.* The *adrogatus* and persons in his power passed under the *potestas* of the *adrogator*. The adrogator's debts were extinguished (*see* XV, **10**) but a Praetorian *actio utilis* (*see* XXII, **6**) allowed a creditor to proceed against the *adrogator*. The property of the *adrogatus* passed to the *adrogator*. (Justinian allowed the *adrogator* only a usufruct in it.) Obligations of the *adrogatus* arising from delict (*see* XIX) remained attached to him.

(b) *Adoptio*

(i) *Before Justinian.* Under the XII Tables (*see* III), it was ruled "Should a father sell his son three times, the son becomes freed from the power of his father." Adoption could be effected by a father fictitiously selling his son three times by a process of mancipation (*see* X, **12**), after which his power over the son ended; the child was thus mancipated to a purchaser and, in a fictitious *in jure cessio* (*see* X, **13**), the magistrate would give the child to the adoptor.

(ii) *Under Justinian.* The earlier forms were abolished and adoption was allowed only by declaration before a magistrate made by the person giving the child, by the adoptor, and the adoptee.

(iii) *Effects.* The adoptee left his original family and entered the family of the adoptor. Justinian allowed this only where the child was adopted by an ascendant—*adoptio plena* (complete adoption). Where the adoptor was not an ascendant the child stayed in his original family, obtaining a mere right of succession on intestacy to his adoptor, and acquiring the duty (which was reciprocal) of support—*adoptio minus plena* (incomplete adoption). Descendants of the adoptee did not pass into the potestas of the adoptor.

NOTE

(i) There were no restrictions on the adoption of *impubes*.

(ii) Since women did not possess *patria potestas*, they could not adopt or adrogate. Under the Empire, women who had lost children were allowed to adopt.

9. By Imperial Rescript. Where Latins or peregrines were allowed a grant of citizenship by imperial rescript, their children already born were declared to be in their *potestas*.

10. Erroris Causae Probatio (Proof of error). Where a Roman citizen had married a peregrine woman in the mistaken belief that she possessed citizenship, their son would not be a Roman citizen. On giving proof of the error, the son and wife became citizens and the son passed under his father's power.

ITS TERMINATION

11. By death. Death of a *paterfamilias* ended his *potestas*. Where a father died, those in his power became *sui juris*; where a grandfather died, unemancipated grandchildren became *sui juris* only where they did not fall, as a result, into the *potestas* of their father.

12. By variations in status.

(a) Where the *paterfamilias* or son was reduced to slavery *patria potestas* came to an end.

(b) Where a daughter passed into the *manus* of her husband, she passed from the *potestas* exercised by the head of her family.

(c) On the adrogation of a *paterfamilias*, his *potestas* over his children ended.

(d) The adoption of a child (except in the case of *adoptio minus plena* (*see* **8** b(iii) above)) ended the *potestas* exercised over him by the head of the family which he was leaving.

(e) Emancipation of the child ended *patria potestas*.

NOTE

(i) Constantine allowed the revocation of emancipation in the case of gross ingratitude by the emancipated child.

(ii) Father and emancipated son had a reciprocal duty of support in the case of poverty.

13. By the attainment of an eminent dignity by the child in power. *Patria potestas* over a child ended when he became, for example, a *flamen Dialis* (priest of Jupiter) or when the daughter became a *virgo Vestalis* (attendant at the shrine of Vesta), or, in the time of Justinian, when the son attained the consulship or the patriciate (counsellors to the Emperor), or became a bishop.

NOTE

(i) A father who exercised *potestas* over his son might, nevertheless, serve under him, *e.g.* on military service.

(ii) The expulsion of a child from the father's house as a punishment did not bring *potestas* to an end.

(iii) The *potestas* of a father over his children did not end as a result of captivity. When he came back from captivity in a foreign country the *potestas* was renewed by *jus postliminii* (*see* VIII, **6**).

PROGRESS TEST 5

1. Define *patria potestas*. (**1**)

2. Explain the following terms: (a) agnates, (b) cognates. (**2**)

3. What is meant by the description of the Roman family as a "monocracy"? (**2**)

4. What were the powers of a *paterfamilias* under the early law? (**2, 3**)

5. Explain (a) *peculium profecticium*, (b) *bona materna*. (**4**)

6. What were the rights of a son in power in his *peculium castrense*? (**4**)

7. How did *patria potestas* come into existence on marriage? (**6**)

8. Outline *adrogatio* as it was before Justinian. (**8**)

9. What were the main effects on the *adrogatus* of *adrogatio*? (**8**)

10. What changes were made by Justinian in the law of *adoptio*? (**8**)

11. What were the effects of *adoptio*? (**8**)

12. Explain (a) *erroris causae probatio*, (b) *adoptio* by rescript. (**9, 10**)

13. Cassius is in the power of his father, Maevius. As a punishment for misbehaviour he is expelled by Maevius from the family home. Does this end the *potestas*? (Note to **13**)

CHAPTER VI

MARRIAGE

ITS NATURE

1. General. A Roman citizen was under a religious duty to marry and beget children in order that the religious rites of the family might be carried on. The essence of the Roman marriage relationship (*matrimonium*) in its legal aspect lay in its social consequences. Custom, rather than law, dictated the nature of this relationship. At a later date, under the influence of Christian beliefs, the legal relationship between husband and wife assumed a greater importance. The act of marriage was generally informal; it sufficed that the spouses created a union intended to last for life and that they had an intention to look upon the union as marriage (*affectio maritalis*).

SPONSALIA

2. Its meaning. *Sponsalia* (betrothal) involved an agreement to marry. It usually took the form of a stipulation (*see* XVI, **26**) between the *paterfamilias* of the bride and the husband, or his *paterfamilias*.

3. In ancient times. *Sponsalia* required a promise in the form of a stipulation by the parties mentioned in **2** above. Money, which could be recovered if the marriage did not take place, was also promised.

4. During the Republic. At a later stage in the Republic, *sponsalia* no longer involved the penalty mentioned in **3** above. It was possible to dissolve the *sponsalia* by a declaration.

5. During the later Empire. It became the custom for the bridegroom to give his intended bride a gift (*arra sponsalicia*) as a guarantee of the betrothal. This had to be returned twofold if the marriage did not take place.

ITS REQUISITES

6. General. Recognition of a marriage depended upon certain factors including age, consent, *conubium*, intention, lack of disqualifications.

7. Age. Husband and wife had to have reached the age of puberty—14 in the case of the male, 12 in the case of the female.

8. Consent. The consent of the *paterfamilias* was essential where either party was in *potestas* (*see* V). If the *paterfamilias* was insane, or in enemy captivity for three years, his consent was not required. The magistrate could order consent where it was withheld without good reason by a *paterfamilias*.

In later law the consent of the spouses became essential and where a spouse was below the age of 25 and not in *potestas*, parental assent was required.

9. Conubium. Parties had to have the legal capacity for marrying. This meant:

(a) They had to be Roman citizens, or peregrines with the right to contract a marriage considered as valid. In the early law, for example, a patrician-plebeian marriage was forbidden.
(b) They had to be outside the prohibited degrees of relationship (*see* **11** below).

10. Intention. Parties had to have an intention to marry (*affectio maritalis*). In some cases the symbolic act of bringing a wife to the husband's house (*ductio in domum maritii*) was held to establish evidence of *affectio maritalis*. At a later date the existence of a written contract of marriage had the same effect.

11. Lack of Disqualifications.

(a) *Blood relationship*. Marriage between parties sharing a blood relationship was invalid. At no time might those with a lineal relationship marry. The law concerning collaterals prohibited marriage to those up to and within the sixth degree; in the classical period, however, a marriage up to the third degree was allowed, *i.e.* brother and sister, uncle and niece, aunt and nephew could not marry. In the second half of the fourth century first cousins were included in the prohibition, but this was repealed by Justinian.

(b) *Relationship by marriage.* Step-parents and step-children, parents-in-law and children-in-law were disqualified from marriage. This was later extended to include the former spouse of a brother or sister.

(c) *Spiritual relationship* (*cognatio spiritualis*). Justinian prohibited the marriage of god-parents with god-children.

(d) *Existing marriage.* An existing lawful marriage prevented either partner entering another marriage relationship. Bigamy was punished.

(e) *Widows.* Where a widow married within ten months of the death of her husband (twelve months in post-classical law), the marriage was not invalidated, but it brought *infamia* upon her.

> NOTE: *Infamia* involved a loss of one's civic reputation and standing. During the Republic an *infamis* was not allowed to hold office, nor was he allowed to act on behalf of another in litigation. *Infamia censoria* was a punishment by the Censors for unworthy behaviour (*see* I, 11) and involved penal taxation and removal from the list of Senators. *Infamia consularis* led to a person's name being removed by the Censor from a list of those who could offer themselves for election to a public office. *Infamia praetoria* resulted from actions involving dishonourable dealings, *e.g.* the breaking of an oath, theft, robbery, bankruptcy, usury.

(f) *Guardians and Wards.* With some few exceptions (*see* note to VII, 12) guardians (and curators in the post-classical era) were not allowed to marry their wards.

(g) *Other Disqualifications.* (i) Imperial decrees prohibited officers stationed in the provinces marrying women living in their provinces. (ii) During the early Empire soldiers on service were forbidden to marry. (iii) The insane were not allowed to marry. (iv) The later law forbade priests and deacons marrying. (v) Under Justinian, marriage was forbidden between an abductor and the person abducted, adulteress and paramour, Christian and Jew.

> NOTE: A marriage between slaves (*contubernium*) possessed no legal validity.

LAWS OF AUGUSTUS

12. Purpose of the Laws. Augustus introduced legislation designed to penalise the celibate and the childless. By *Lex Julia de maritandis ordinibus* (18 B.C.) and *Lex Papia Poppaea* (A.D. 9) penalties and restrictions were imposed on certain categories of persons.

13. Their nature. Single men of 25–60, and women of 20–50, and divorced or widowed persons in those age groups, were placed under a duty to marry. *Jus liberorum* exempted a freeman with three legitimate children, and a freedman with four children. By this legislation an unmarried man could not take under a will, and married persons with no children could take only one half of any legacy left to them. A freeborn citizen was not allowed to marry an actress or a prostitute or a procuress.

NOTE: These laws were abolished gradually, or became obsolete, in the fourth and fifth centuries.

FORMS OF MARRIAGE

14. Manus Marriage (*manus* = hand).

(a) *Its nature.* By this form of marriage, a woman was transferred from her family to the family of her husband and was said to be "in his hand" (*in manum viri*).

(b) *Its modes.*

    (i) *Confarreatio* (*far* = spelt cake). This ceremony was confined to the patricians. Spelt bread was used in a sacrificial ceremony to Jupiter, which took place in the presence of the *flamen Dialis* (a high priest) and ten witnesses.

    (ii) *Coemptio.* By a type of mancipation (*see* X, **12**), power over the woman was transferred to the husband in return for a symbolic payment by the *paterfamilias* in the presence of five witnesses.

    (iii) *Usus.* No special ceremony was held and cohabitation for one year sufficed to bring the wife under the *manus* of her husband.

(c) *Its effects.* The wife came under the *potestas* (*see* V) of the head of her husband's family. Her property passed to her husband and any property acquired thereafter also passed to him. A husband was responsible for his wife's obligations to the extent of her property. Having passed into the *manus* of her husband, her position approximated to that of his daughter; if her husband was in the power of his father she stood in the relationship of a grand-daughter to the father.

NOTE

    (i) In the case of *usus* (*see* **14**(b)(iii) above), a wife who stayed away from her husband for three consecutive nights (*trinoctii absentia*) did not pass under his *manus*, according to the law of the XII Tables.

   (ii) These modes of marriage had disappeared by the end of the second century A.D.

15. Free Marriage.

(a) *Its nature.* A valid marriage could be made without any ceremony where the essentials of marriage existed (*see* **6** above).

(b) *Its modes.* No specific mode was necessary.

(c) *Its effects.* The wife did not pass into the *manus* of her husband. In the absence of *dos* (*see* **26** below), she had no rights to maintenance by her husband, but her property remained her own.

CONCUBINAGE

16. Its nature. Concubinage was the term applied to a permanent union between a man and woman which lacked *affectio maritalis*, *i.e.* the parties had no intention of marrying. Parties to this relationship had to be of marriageable age and had to be outside the prohibited relationships (*see* **11** above). It was forbidden for a man to have both a wife and a concubine, or two concubines; nor was he allowed to take another man's wife as his concubine.

17. Children. A child born in concubinage was illegitimate. It was considered as a cognate of the mother and could be legitimated (*see* **29** below).

DISSOLUTION OF MARRIAGE

18. Death. Marriage was dissolved by death. In some cases a widow was not free to remarry immediately (*see* **11**(e) above).

19. Prolonged absence. This could have the same effect as death on marriage. The absence of news from a spouse for a considerable period, and circumstances from which death might be presumed could end a marriage.

20. Enslavement. The enslavement of a spouse by *jus civile* (*see* VIII, **7**) terminated the marriage.

21. Incestus Superveniens. If, for example, a father (A) adopted the wife (B) of his son (C), or the husband (D) of his daughter (E), the marriages between B and C, and D and E were considered as dissolved.

22. Divorce.

(a) *In manus marriage. Confarreatio* marriage (*see* **14**(b)(i) above) could be dissolved by *diffarreatio*; *coemptio* or *usus* marriage (*see* **14**(b)(ii) and (iii) above) could be dissolved by *remancipatio*, by which the wife was transferred to her former *paterfamilias*.

(b) *In free marriage.* It was possible for a father to take back his daughter against her wishes or her husband's. Antoninus Pius prohibited this. Divorce by mutual consent was possible in free marriage.

(c) *Under Constantine and Justinian.* Under Constantine divorce was allowed for specified reasons, *e.g.*, misconduct of a spouse. Divorce without reasonable cause was penalised. In A.D. 542 Justinian prohibited divorce by mutual consent, except where the husband was impotent, or wished to enter a monastery, or where either spouse was in captivity.

(d) *Formalities.* No particular form was needed for a *repudium* (declaration of divorce). The *Lex Julia de adulteriis* (18 B.C.) required that a *repudium* be delivered by a freedman in the presence of seven adult Roman citizens.

MATRIMONIAL PROPERTY

23. Gifts between spouses. These were prohibited, not only between the spouses, but among all members of the two families. Where such a gift was made, the transaction was void and the gift remained in the ownership of the donor. This prohibition did not apply:

(a) In the case of a present involving moderate expense only.
(b) In the case of customary gifts. A *senatusconsultum* in the time of Caracalla enacted that such a gift should be revocable during the marriage, or if the donee died before the donor, or if the marriage were dissolved by divorce.
(c) In the case of a gift for maintenance.
(d) In the case of gifts made in contemplation of divorce or death, to take effect in those events.

> NOTE: Where there was a question as to the source of particular property possessed by the wife, the *praesumptio Muciana* (named after Q. Mucius Scaevola, 59 B.C.) allowed a presumption (in absence of proof to the contrary) that it had been given to her by her husband.

24. Donatio ante Nuptias (Gift before marriage). This took the form of a settlement on the wife made by the husband and intended as his share of the expenses of the marriage. So that the prohibition in **23** above might not take effect, the *donatio* was made before the marriage. On the husband's death, or in the case of divorce without fault on the wife's part, the *donatio* passed to her. If there were children, they received the ownership of the donatio and the wife received a usufruct (*see* XI, **9**) in it.

25. Donatio propter Nuptias (Gift on account of marriage). Under Justinian a settlement might be made before or after the marriage. There was rarely a transfer of property; the husband merely contracted to make a gift.

26. Dos. This was a gift of anything possessing monetary value made (often by a written document—*instrumentum dotale*) by the wife, or someone on her behalf, to the matrimonial expenses.

(a) *Methods of constituting a dos.* A *dos* could be constituted by: *Dotis Promissio*—a promise to give *dos* (*see* also XVIII **6**(b)); *Dotis Dictio*—a verbal contract to give *dos*; *Dotis Datio*—a conveyance of *dos* so that it was vested in the husband.
(b) *Types of dos.* *Dos profecticia* was given by the wife's father,

or her *paterfamilias*; *Dos adventicia* was given by any other
person; *dos recepticia* was given with the stipulation that it
was to be returned to the donor if and when the marriage
was dissolved.

(c) *Ownership and devolution of dos.* (i) In pre-classical times
dos vested absolutely in the husband and it did not revert,
unless *dos recepticia*, when it reverted on agreed terms.
(ii) During the classical period an *actio ex stipulatu* enabled
the wife to reclaim *dos* in the event of divorce or her husband's death. The *actio rei uxoriae* allowed her to reclaim
a portion of the *dos*, in the event of divorce, subject to the
retention by the husband of one-sixth for each child and a
further sixth if the wife had been the guilty party. On the
wife's death, the donor could recover the *dos* where such a
right had been stipulated, but the husband was allowed to
retain one-fifth for each child (*see* also XI, 2(a)). By juristic
interpretation non-fungible objects (*see* IX, 13) were to be
restored as soon as the marriage ended; fungible objects
could be restored in three annual instalments. Where dotal
property had been destroyed or damaged, the husband was
liable for *culpa* (negligence) or *dolus* (fraud, bad faith).
(iii) Under Justinian the *dos* went to the wife on the death
of her husband, or on divorce if she was not the guilty
party. On her death (where she was not in power) the husband was given a usufruct in the *dos*, the ownership of
which was vested in the children. In the event of divorce
in which the wife was a guilty party, the husband kept the
dos. Deductions (*see* (ii) above) were abolished. The *actio
dotis* gave the wife a hypothec (*see* XI, 16) over the husband's property as security for the return of the *dos*. In
A.D. 531, Justinian forbade the alienation or hypotheca-
tion of dotal immovables.

CHILDREN

27. Their legal condition.

(a) In general, the children of a legal marriage followed the
status possessed by their father at the time of their conception.

(b) Children who were born out of civil wedlock followed the
status of the mother at the time of conception.

(c) A child born from a marriage between a peregrine and a Roman citizen followed the status possessed by the father at its conception, if the peregrine possessed *conubium* (*see* **9** above). If the peregrine lacked *conubium*, the child followed the mother's status. A *Lex Minicia* (from before 90 B.C.) ruled that such a child would be a peregrine, no matter what the status of its mother. In this matter Latins were considered as peregrines; Junian Latins (*see* VIII, **10**(c)) were not (*see* also V, **10**).

28. Illegitimate children. An illegitimate child (*spurius*) was born *sui juris* and had a cognatic relationship with its mother. As in the case of legitimate children, illegitimate children and their mother had a reciprocal duty of support. They could succeed to their mother on intestacy.

29. Legitimation. Children born in concubinage (*see* **16** above), known as *liberi naturales*, could be legitimated in the following ways:

(a) *By Imperial Rescript.* Justinian allowed this if there were no legitimate children and marriage had become impossible (because, for example, the mother had died). *Legitimatio per rescriptum principis* was also possible where a father, in his will, desired that his children should become legitimate; in this case the children had a right to apply for the rescript.

(b) *By subsequent marriage (legitimatio per subsequens matrimonium).* Justinian allowed this subject to the child's consent and the existence of a correctly formulated marriage contract, or the existence of a settlement of *dos* (*see* **26** above). Additionally, the child's parents had to prove that they were capable of a legal marriage at the time of the child's conception.

(c) *By offering to a Municipal Council (legitimatio per oblationem curiae).* Where a natural son was provided with property by his father to enable him to become a member of a municipal council (*decurio*), or where a natural daughter was provided with property so as to marry a *decurio*, the son and daughter were legitimated. This method of legitimation, introduced by Theodosius and Valentinian, originated in attempts to fill an expensive and burdensome public office.

NOTE: Justinian allowed to *liberi naturales* and their mother a right of succession in one-sixth of the property on the father's intestacy, but only where neither a wife nor legitimate children had a right of succession. A father was allowed to leave property by will to his concubine and her children.

PROGRESS TEST 6

1. Give an account of the meaning and significance of *sponsalia*. (**2-5**)

2. What were the requirements for a valid marriage? (**6-11**)

3. Was a valid marriage possible between Cominius and Virgilia, both aged 13? (**7**)

4. What was meant by *conubium*? (**9**)

5. Could a valid marriage take place in the following cases?
   (a) Virgilia is 15; Cominius is aged 17. Cominius is in the *potestas* of Casca, who refuses his consent to the marriage.
   (b) Casca, aged 45, wishes to marry his ward, Portia, aged 19. (**8, 11**)

6. Explain (a) *affectio maritalis*, (b) *cognatio spiritualis*. (**10, 11**)

7. Outline the marriage laws of Augustus. (**12, 13**)

8. What were the main differences between free marriage and other forms of marriage? (**14, 15**)

9. What was the nature of *manus* marriage? How did it take place? (**14**)

10. Explain (a) *trinoctii absentia*, (b) *contubernium*. (**11, 14**)

11. Define concubinage. What was the status of a child born in concubinage? (**16, 17**)

12. What was the effect on marriage of a prolonged absence of the husband? (**19**)

13. How was *manus* marriage dissolved? (**22**)

14. Was misconduct of a spouse sufficient cause for divorce under Justinian? (**22**)

15. What were the exceptions to the rule against gifts between spouses? (**23**)

16. Explain the nature of *donatio ante nuptias*. (**24**)

17. What were the methods by which *dos* could be constituted? (**26**)

18. Outline the conditions of ownership and devolution of *dos* during the classical period. (**26**)

19. What was the status of a child born, in 100 B.C., from a marriage between a *civis Romanus* and a peregrine woman? (**27**)

20. Explain *legitimatio per oblationem curiae*. (**29**)

CHAPTER VII

TUTORS AND CURATORS

LEGAL CAPACITY

1. Of Children. The stages in a child's life were considered under Roman Law to be as follows:

(a) *Infantia* (*infancy*). The child is unable to speak properly and, hence, is lacking in *intellectus* (intelligence) and *judicium* (powers of judgment). Children at this stage were considered to be without legal capacity.

(b) *Infantiae Proximus* (next to infancy). The child, at this stage was able to speak, but was lacking in *intellectus* and *judicium*. At the time of the later Empire, *intellectus* was presumed to exist at seven years of age, at which *infantia* ceased.

(c) *Pubertati Proximus* (next to puberty). The child lacked *judicium*, but could perform transactions which bound another party, although he was unable to bind himself without *auctoritas tutoris* (the authority of his *tutor*—*see* **7** below).

(d) *Pubertas* (puberty): 14 (male), or 12 (female). At this age full legal capacity was assumed.

> NOTE: The jurists, prior to Justinian, had differed as to the test for determining the puberty of a male. The Proculians, for example (*see* II, **19**), had suggested the age of 14; the Sabinians had thought that age should be determined solely by physical capacity (*habitu corporis*).

2. Of Women. Roman Law did not grant women equality with men. Women were not allowed to participate in public life and could not hold public office. They were not allowed to adopt and, in earlier times and in the classical period, they could not enter formal transactions without a tutor's authority (*see* **11** below).

3. Of Prodigals. The *prodigus* (spendthrift) possessed full legal powers. But a Praetorian interdiction prevented him from dissipating his property if it might have resulted in his children's reduction to poverty. During the classical period this applied to any dealings which might have been detrimental to his own property. The *prodigus* was obliged to have a *curator* (*see* **15** below).

4. Of Lunatics. *Furiosi* (*furor* = lunacy) lacked full legal capacity although, following the classical period, a contract entered into by a *furiosus* during a lucid interval was held to be valid. The *furiosus* required a *curator* (*see* **16** below).

TUTELA IMPUBERUM

5. Its nature. *Tutela Impuberum* (tutelage of young persons under puberty) applied to *impubes* who were not subject to *patria potestas* (*see* V). A *tutor* (*tueri* = to protect) possessed powers analogous to those of a contemporary trustee over his ward and the ward's property. Where the ward (*pupillus*) lacked full capacity for legal acts, the *tutor* had the power (and sometimes the responsibility) to make good the deficiency. As in the case of a trustee, the exercise of *tutela* meant that the *tutor* could not charge for his services, could not enrich himself from his relationship with the ward, and had to make good any losses arising from his neglect or default. Because *tutela* was a *publicum munus* (public duty) it was obligatory on those nominated. (For the exceptions see **9** below).

6. Types of tutor.

(a) *Tutor Testamentarius* (*appointed by name in the will of a paterfamilias*). This *tutor* would exercise tutelage over sons who were in *potestas* and under the age of puberty and who would become *sui juris* (*see* IV, **4**) on the death of the *paterfamilias*. Tutelage commenced as soon as the will took effect. Until the time of Claudius the *tutor* so nominated could refuse; after Claudius he could apply for exemption only on specified grounds (*see* **9** below).

(b) *Tutor Legitimus* (*appointed by operation of law*).

  (i) *Legitima Tutela Agnatorum.* Under the XII Tables, where there was no *tutor testamentarius*, tutelage would fall on the nearest agnates.
      EXAMPLE: Sempronius is father of Titius and Maevius

(both above the age of puberty) and Brutus, aged 6. The death of Sempronius releases his sons from *patria potestas*. Sempronius does not nominate a *tutor* for Brutus in his will. Titius and Maevius would become the joint statutory tutors. The next agnates on whom the statutory tutorship would fall are the brothers of Sempronius.

NOTE: Justinian, by *Novella* 118, gave *tutela* to the next of kin whether cognatic or agnatic.

(ii) *Legitima Tutela Parentum.* When a paterfamilias emancipated a descendant below the age of puberty he became its *tutor*.

(iii) *Legitima Tutela Patronorum.* When a master manumitted a slave (*see* VIII, 9) below the age of puberty he became its *tutor*.

(c) *Tutor Fiduciarius.* This term had two meanings:

(i) Where a father died after emancipating a child below the age of puberty, the unemancipated brothers of the child became its *fiduciary tutors*.

(ii) Where a child below the age of puberty was emancipated and had not been re-mancipated to the father but was manumitted by a third party, that party became its *fiduciary tutor*.

(d) *Tutor Dativus.* In some cases a tutor might be appointed by decree, *e.g.* in default of other appointments, and where the child needed a *tutor*, any person might apply; the child's mother was under a duty to apply. *Lex Atilia* (*c.* 200 B.C.) gave the Praetor Urbanus (*see* I, 11) and the plebeian Tribunes the power to appoint tutors in Rome in these circumstances. *Lex Julia et Titia* (31 B.C.) gave this power to provincial governors. Under Claudius, Consuls, and in post-classical times, governors of cities, were given the power of appointment.

NOTE: A temporary *tutor* might be appointed for a particular matter, *e.g.* a *tutor praetorius*, appointed specially to act for a *pupillus* involved in litigation with his *tutor*.

7. Tasks and Functions of the Tutor.

(a) *Administration of the ward's property* (*negotia gerere*). Where possible, the money belonging to the *pupillus* had to be invested so as to produce interest. (Justinian allowed the money to be hoarded, unless used for the maintenance of the *pupillus*.) The ward's debts had to be settled, perishable things had to be sold and, in the post-classical era, an inventory of the estate had to be made. By an *oratio* (*see* II, 20) of Septimius Severus in A.D. 195, a transaction involving the sale of undeveloped building land and agricultural land belonging to the *pupillus* was forbidden; this was extended by Constantine to all valuable movables, unless authorised by will or a magistrate's decree. In these matters the *tutor* had to show *maxima diligentia* (the utmost care) and had to perform his duties as a *bonus paterfamilias* might have performed them.

(b) *Interposition of his authority* (*auctoritatem interponere*). Where the *pupillus* had *intellectus* only, the *tutor* could make good the lack of *judicium* and thus make an incomplete transaction effective. This allowed a *pupillus* to make a contract in his own name. No liability could be incurred without the authority of a *tutor*. This *auctoritas* had to be given at the time of the act and by the *tutor* in person, not by his agent. Where a ward had become enriched from a contract concluded without his tutor's authority, he was liable, by a rescript of Antoninus Pius, in an *actio utilis*, to restore the amount of his enrichment. If the creditor of a *pupillus*, in ignorance of his lack of capacity, accepted payment and used the money, the debt was held to be extinguished.

(c) *Education of the ward.* The *tutor* was bound, not to bring up the ward, but to provide for his education. He was bound to make an annual appearance in court so that a sum might be fixed for this purpose. The sum, paid out of the estate of the *pupillus*, was given to those who were bringing him up.

8. Protection of the Pupillus.

(a) A *tutor legitimus* or *dativus* was obliged to take an oath to administer the property of the *pupillus* with care, and this oath was backed by security—*satisdatio rem pupilli salvam fore*. A magistrate who omitted to obtain this security was liable in damages (*see* XVI, 31). A *tutor* appointed by will was not obliged to give security.

(b) Tutors were appointed by magistrates only after an inquiry as to their suitability; the magistrate was responsible in damages for an unsatisfactory nomination.

(c) In the post-classical era, the *tutor* was obliged to make an inventory of the property before commencing his duties.

(d) At the end of the tutorship an *actio rationibus distrahendis* ("for the taking apart of the accounts") could be brought against a *tutor legitimus*. Twofold damages could be claimed for the embezzlement of property belonging to the *pupillus*.

(e) A *tutor* could be removed for actual or anticipated misconduct. An *actio suspecti tutoris* could be brought in a case of fraud or extreme negligence in carrying out the tutor's duties. Condemnation brought *infamia* (*see* VI, **11**(e)).

(f) An *oratio* of Septimius Severus (see **7**(a) above) forbade the sale of immovable property without authorisation by will or by a magistrate.

(g) In the later Republic an *actio tutelae* could be brought for *dolus* (fraud) and *culpa* (negligence). An *actio contraria tutelae* allowed a *tutor* to recover legitimate expenses incurred in administering the property of the *pupillus*.

(h) Constantine introduced a *hypotheca* (mortgage—*see* XI, **16**) over the tutor's property to secure any claim made by the *pupillus*.

NOTE: A *tutor* was allowed to buy from his ward when the sale was of a part of the property which the *tutor* was not managing.

9. Excusationes Tutorum (exceptions from tutorship). Because of the obligatory nature of tutorship there arose a large number of exceptions from tutorship, *e.g.* infirmity; old age (over 70); long distance of tutor's residence from the *pupillus*; the holding of other tutorships; poverty; illiteracy; military service; enmity between the *tutor* and the father of the *pupillus*; an appointment made from ill-will; absence on state business; holding a high public office (*e.g.* Treasury official); membership of certain professions (*e.g.* medicine); inequality of rank (*e.g.* a Senator was exempted from acting as a *tutor*, except to another Senator's children).

NOTE

(i) Marcus Aurelius gave the Praetor Tutelarius the right to decide whether a ground of excuse was valid.

    (ii) In the classical period a *tutor dativus* could, by *potioris nominatio*, ask to name a more appropriate person. This right disappeared under Justinian.

    (iii) Slaves, peregrines, those under 25, the deaf and dumb, monks and bishops, were not allowed to act as tutors. Women were also disqualified, but Justinian allowed a tutorship to widowed mothers who promised not to re-marry.

10. Cessation of Tutelage. Tutelage came to an end in the following ways:

(a) When the *pupillus* reached the age of puberty.

(b) When the *tutor* or *pupillus* died.

(c) When the *tutor* retired, having been discharged by a magistrate.

(d) Where a *tutor* had been appointed until a certain time, or pending a condition, and the time expired or the condition was fulfilled.

(e) Where a *tutor* had been removed because of suspected or actual misconduct, or hostility to the ward.

(f) Where either party suffered *capitis deminutio* (*see* IV, 6).

    EXAMPLES:

    (i) Marcus is *tutor* to Stichus. Stichus is given in adoption to Gaius. The tutorship of Marcus comes to an end.

    (ii) Veratius is *tutor* to Brutus and is captured by enemy forces and taken into captivity. The tutorship of Veratius thereby comes to an end.

TUTELA PERPETUA MULIERUM

11. Its significance and development

(a) Women, even in the classical period, did not possess full legal capacity. A woman who was *sui juris* was, therefore, under *tutela perpetua mulierum* (perpetual tutelage of women), as contrasted with the temporary tutelage of the *impubes*.

(b) The function of the *tutor* was confined to *auctoritatem interponere* (*see* 7(b) above). This function was exercised when the woman wished to contract a legal obligation or to sell *res mancipi* (*see* IX, 6). In classical times the Praetor would compel an unwilling *tutor* to give *auctoritas* in an appropriate case.

(c) A woman under tutelage could often choose her *tutor*, and was allowed to change her *tutor* by an action based on *in jure cessio* (*see* X, **13**).

(d) *Tutela perpetua* was modified before Justinian, under whom it was applied only to women under the age of puberty. In A.D. 9 *Leges Julia et Papia Poppaea* gave the *jus liberorum* to a freeborn woman with three children and to a freedwoman with four children. They were also freed from the requirement of *tutela*. Claudius abolished the tutorship of agnates for women of full age. In A.D. 410 Theodosius granted *jus liberorum* to all women (*see* also note to XII, **19**).

12. Types of tutor

(a) *Tutor Testamentarius*. A testator could allow the woman to choose her *tutor* (*tutor optivus*). At one time the practice existed of leaving the tutor's name in a will as a blank and allowing the woman to insert a name.

(b) *Tutor Legitimus*. As in the case of *tutela impuberum*, the tutelage fell upon the woman's nearest agnates.

(c) *Tutor Dativus*. As in the case of *tutela impuberum* (*see* **6**(d) above).

NOTE: Tutors were not generally allowed to marry wards. There was an exception if they had been betrothed before the *tutor* had taken office, or if the ward was 25, or if the Emperor had given his permission.

CURA

13. Its nature. *Cura* (guardianship over minors) arose with the realisation that a child who had reached puberty was, nevertheless, too young to administer its affairs. Those who dealt with minors might be at a disadvantage (*see* **14** below). The function of the *curator* was primarily to administer the property of the minor; he had no control over the person of the minor. The *curator* was expected to give his approval (*consensus*) to transactions of a reasonable nature which the minor wished to undertake.

14. Cura Minorum (curatorship of minors).

(a) *A person reached perfecta aetas* at the age of 25, at which he had full capacity to act on his own behalf without the consent of a *tutor* or a *curator*. Caracalla introduced *venia aetatis*, a dispensation by which males of 20 and females of 18 were allowed to manage their own affairs without the assistance of a *curator* in certain circumstances, *e.g.* to administer the affairs of a dead parent. This dispensation did not extend to the selling of land, which required the court's permission.

(b) *Lex Plaetoria* (200 B.C.) punished anyone who fraudulently over-reached a person under 25. The Praetorian Interdict *restitutio in integrum* (*see* XXIII, **17**) provided for the rescission of a transaction to which the minor had been a party, and a restoration to his former position, if he had suffered damage in the transaction as a result of his lack of judgment. It was not necessary to prove fraud in this case. Hence, persons must have feared dealing with minors.

(c) Originally a *curator* was appointed to act in single transactions on the application of the minor. Later, the magistrates appointed a *curator* on an application from any person who wished to complete a transaction with a minor. Under Marcus Aurelius the curatorship continued throughout the entire period of minority. Under Diocletian a minor seems to have been without capacity; he could not engage in any transaction likely to worsen his position unless his *curator* had given *consensus*.

NOTE

(i) During the Republic the consensus of the *curator* could be of an informal nature and signified merely that he considered the transaction to be proper.

(ii) A *tutor* to a female aged 12–25 had no powers to administer her affairs (*see* **11**(b) above); hence she might need a *curator* and a *tutor*.

(iii) The *actio negotiorum gestorum* was available for claims between *curator* and minor.

15. Cura Prodigi (curatorship of the spendthrift) (*see* **3** above). A spendthrift was prevented by Praetorian Interdict from wasting his property. The relatives of such a person could apply for the appointment of a *curator* who would be responsible for managing the property and whose *consensus* would be needed for any act which might result in liability attaching to the *prodigus*.

16. Cura Furiosi (curatorship of the lunatic) (*see* **4** above). Under the XII Tables the agnates and then the *gentiles* (members of the clan to which the *furiosus* belonged) had the power of *cura* over the *furiosus*. The *curator* had power of administration over his property and was obliged to take care of him. Under Justinian a hypothec over the curator's property was demanded. A *curator* was obliged to make an inventory of the lunatic's property.

17. Other curatorships. The magistrates had the power to appoint curators to the following persons: the deaf, dumb, and infirm; a *pupillus* temporarily without a *tutor*; a child *en ventre sa mère*; those suffering from an incurable disease.

18. Cessation of cura. A curatorship came to an end when the minor reached the age of 25, or by *venia aetatis* (*see* **14**(a) above), or by misconduct of the *curator* resulting in his removal from the position.

NOTE: In post-classical times the *excusationes* for a *tutor* (*see* **9** above) were extended to a *curator*.

PROGRESS TEST 7

1. Explain the terms (a) *infantia*, (b) *pubertas*. (**1**)
2. What was the general legal status of the *prodigus*? (**3**)
3. Outline the nature of *tutela impuberum*. (**5**)
4. What was a *tutor testamentarius*? What were his duties? (**6**)
5. Explain (a) *legitima tutela agnatorum*, (b) *legitima tutela parentum*. (**6**)
6. Under what circumstances could a *tutor* be appointed by decree? (**6**)
7. What were the main functions of a *tutor*? (**7**)
8. In what cases was a *tutor* obliged to give security? (**8**)
9. What was the *actio rationibus distrahendis*? (**8**)
10. After the reign of Claudius, Menenius is appointed *tutor testamentarius*. On what grounds could he claim exemption from taking up the appointment? (**9**)
11. What was the effect on tutelage of *capitis deminutio*? (**10**)
12. On what grounds could an *actio suspecti tutoris* be brought? (**8**)
13. Why was *tutela perpetua mulierum* considered necessary? (**11**)

14. Explain the nature of *cura*. **(13)**

15. Define (a) *perfecta aetas*, (b) *venia aetatis*. **(14)**

16. Under what circumstances could the magistrates appoint a *curator*? **(14)**

17. When did a curatorship end? **(18)**

CHAPTER VIII

SLAVERY

ITS NATURE

1. The Slave: person or thing? Slavery was recognised as a part of *jus gentium* (*see* II, **8**) since it was practised and recognised by many peoples other than the Romans, but it was not considered part of *jus naturale* (*see* II, **7**) since men were free by nature. Slaves (*servi* or *mancipia*) were owned by their masters and did not possess either private or public rights. Their masters possessed absolute rights over them (*see* **4** below). The slave was a *res* (a thing), and yet a person. As a *res* his master owned him and could sell him; as a person he was subject to the criminal law and could gain his freedom.

2. Freeborn and freemade persons. It is important to note the following distinction: a man who was not enslaved was either *ingenuus* (freeborn) or *libertinus* (freemade). The *ingenuus* was born of free parents, the *libertinus* had been manumitted from enslavement (*see* also **12** below).

NOTE

(i) Large numbers of slaves were brought to Rome as a result of Roman conquests. Their conditions were often very bad, usually much worse in the country than in the towns; a slave might be punished by being sent into the country. Slaves were often subjected to harsh and cruel treatment at the whims of their masters.

(ii) The *actio liberalis causa* (action for liberty) could be brought to decide whether, in fact, a person was free or enslaved.

LEGAL STATUS OF THE SLAVE

3. Lack of rights.

(a) Since the slave possessed none of the *tria capita—familia, civitas, libertas* (*see* IV, **6**)—he lacked legal rights.

(b) *Because he had no property rights*, that which he acquired went to his master. But a master could allow his slave a *peculium* (a small amount of private property) which was looked upon (but not recognised by law) as being the slave's property, although the master could retake it at any time. A slave was allowed to make a loan to a person, but, in such a case, the slave's master became the creditor. A slave might act as his master's representative in certain transactions and, in such a case, Praetorian *actiones adjecticiae qualitatis* (*see* XVII, **25**(c))—actions of a supplementary nature—were available against the master in respect of the slave's obligations. Slaves who traded by using their *peculium* were allowed *administratio peculii*: they could sell, pledge, pay debts, but could not make gifts with it.

(c) In some cases a master could enforce an agreement of a contractual nature made by his slave (*see* XVI, **34**).

(d) With very few exceptions no slave could be a party to civil actions.

(e) Marriages between slaves were not recognised by law.

4. Subject to his master.

(a) In the early law the slave was subject to *vitae necisque potestas* (the power of life and death) exercised by his master. For modifications to this absolute power *see* **8** below.

(b) Noxal surrender of slaves by their masters could be made following an *actio noxalis* (*see* XX, **6–7**).

> NOTE: During the Empire many slaves were given work of responsibility to the State. They were known as *Servi Publici Populi Romani* and were given certain privileges, *e.g.* the right to dispose by will of one-half of *peculium*.

CAUSES OF ENSLAVEMENT

5. General. Enslavement arose under Roman Law

(a) by *jus gentium* (*see* II, **8**), or,

(b) by *jus civile* (*see* II, **10**).

6. Enslavement by Jus Gentium

(a) *Enslavement by descent.* By *jus gentium* a child followed the status of its mother at the time it was born. Hence the child of a slave-mother was a slave.

NOTE: A *favor libertatis* provided an exception to this and allowed freedom to a child born to a slave-mother who had been free for any period of time during pregnancy.

(b) *Enslavement by capture in time of war.* Since enemies were generally put to death or considered as slaves of their conquerors, a Roman who was captured by hostile armies was considered a slave.

NOTE: *Jus Postliminii* (*post limen* = across the threshold) restored rights to a captive who returned to his home with the intention of resuming those rights. *Postliminium* did not apply where the captive returned during a period of armistice or where he had surrendered or deserted to the enemy. His rights were considered as in suspension during the period of captivity; these rights were considered as having ended at the time of his capture in the event of his dying as a captive.

7. Enslavement by Jus Civile.

(a) *A manifest thief* (*see* XIX, 12) could be enslaved under the early law.

(b) *A person who evaded military service*, or taxation, or the census, could be enslaved.

(c) *A woman could be enslaved if she cohabited with a slave* whose master had forbidden this. The children of such a union would be slaves (*see* also XIV, 20).

(d) *Servi poenae, i.e.* those condemned to death, or to enforced labour in the mines, or to a contest with wild beasts in the arena, were considered enslaved.

(e) *A libertinus* (*see* 2 above) *guilty of ingratitude* to his patron (*see* 12 below) could be returned to slavery.

(f) *An insolvent debtor* might be sold "across the Tiber", *i.e.* into foreign slavery, under the early law.

(g) *A man over twenty years of age* who had allowed himself to be sold as a slave, with fraudulent intent, could be enslaved as a punishment.

(h) *A child could be sold as a slave by parents* in great poverty, but a right of redemption existed.

(i) *Dediticii* (whose ancestors had been the inhabitants of states conquered and destroyed by the Romans) were not allowed to reside within one hundred miles of Rome on penalty of being reduced to slavery.

NOTE: Justinian abolished (c) and (d) as causes of slavery.

PROTECTION OF THE SLAVE

8. Stages in Legislation. Entirely without rights, the slave in early law could be put to death at the will of his master. Later legislation shielded him to some extent from unrestrained cruelty.

(a) *Lex Cornelia de Sicariis* (82 B.C.) made the killing of another's slave without lawful reason a capital offence.

(b) *Lex Petronia* (c. A.D. 78) prohibited the punishment of exposure of a slave to combat in the arena with wild beasts without a magistrate's permission.

(c) *Claudius* gave freedom (with Latin rights—*see* **10**(c) below) to a slave who had been abandoned because of infirmity.

(d) *Hadrian* prohibited a master putting his slave to death without a magistrate's permission. He also forbade the castration of a slave. *Ergastula* (houses of correction for slaves) were abolished.

(e) *Antoninus Pius* brought the killing by a master of his own slave within *Lex Cornelia de Sicariis* (*see* (a) above). He also enacted that a slave who, because of his master's cruelty, had sought protection in a temple, was to be sold to another master.

(f) *Constantine and Justinian* allowed a master to inflict only moderate chastisement as punishment for a slave.

TERMINATION OF ENSLAVEMENT

9. Manumission. Manumission—a voluntary act by a master which had the effect of liberating his slave—took a variety of forms.

(a) *Legitima Manumissio* (formal manumission) was effected in three ways:

  (i) *Testamento.* A grant of freedom by will. It was essential that the slave belonged to the testator at the time of making the will and at the time of death. The slave became the testator's freedman—*libertus orcinus* (*orcinus* = relating to the dead)—and rights of patronage over him (*see* **12** below) vested in the testator's family. A testator could also request his heir to manumit a slave. The heir was obliged to carry out such a request and, on doing so, he became the patron of the freed slave.

(ii) *Censu* (by census). The master would enrol his slave as a free person during the census which took place every five years. The last census was taken in A.D. 74, and this method of manumission became obsolete during the Republic.

(iii) *Per Vindictam* (*vindicta* = a wand). This was a fictitious suit in which the master, slave, and a third party (*adsertor libertatis*) appeared before the Praetor. The *adsertor* touched the slave with a wand and claimed him as a free person. The master assented and the slave was declared to be free. The master had to have full ownership of the slave in civil law and had to appear personally—he could not be represented in the proceedings.

(b) *Manumissio minus solemnis* (manumission in the informal mode). This could be carried out in several ways:

(i) *In sacrosanctis ecclesiis*. Manumission might be performed, in the later law, in the presence of a Christian bishop and his congregation. This mode was introduced by Constantine.

(ii) *Per mensam* (or *convivii adhibitione*). The slave was summoned to his master's table and manumitted.

(iii) *Per epistolam*. The slave's freedom was granted by letter.

(iv) *Inter amicos*. A statement of the slave's having been set free was made in the presence of a group of the master's friends.

(v) *By appointment of a slave* as one's heir, or as the tutor of one's son or by adopting him as one's son. These modes of manumission were introduced by Justinian.

NOTE: In general, *manumissio minus solemnis* had little effect; the manumitted slave had no protection if his master died. At a later date, the slave manumitted informally was said to be *in libertate*; he had no proprietary rights, but enjoyed personal freedom (*see* also *Lex Junia*—**10**(c) below).

10. Legislation concerning manumission.

(a) *Lex Fufia Caninia* (2 B.C.) limited manumission by will. An owner of 2 slaves might free them both in this way; an owner of 2–10 slaves could manumit only half of them; from 10–30, one-third; from 30–100, one-fourth; from 100–500, one-fifth. More than one hundred slaves belonging to one master could not be manumitted in this way. The *Lex* was repealed by Justinian.

(b) *Lex Aelia Sentia* (A.D. 4). The main provisions of this important legislation were:

    (i) Any attempt at manumission by a master under twenty years of age was void, unless approved by a special council (*Consilium*). Where such approval was given, and the manumission had been *per vindictam* (*see* **9**(a)(iii) above), the slave became a citizen. If the manumission had been informal he became a Junian Latin (*see* (c) below).

    (ii) A manumission intended to defraud a creditor was void, as was a manumission carried out by an insolvent master.

    (iii) The approval of the *Consilium* was needed for manumission of a slave under 30. Without such approval, the slave became a Junian Latin.

    (iv) *Anniculi probatio* was introduced, as a result of which a Junian Latin under 30 who married another Junian Latin, or a citizen, in the presence of seven witnesses, could achieve citizenship one year after the birth of a child, where these facts were proved before a magistrate.

    (v) A grant of citizenship could not be made to a slave who had been punished for a grave crime; he could achieve no more than the status of the *dediticii* (*see* **7** (i) above).

> NOTE: Most of the above sections of the *Lex* were repealed by Justinian, but he gave a right of manumission by will to masters at the age of 17, and, later, of 14.

(c) *Lex Junia Norbana* (date unknown, perhaps *c.* A.D. 19). Some of Rome's Latin neighbours were known as *Latini Coloniarii*. They had freedom, but their rights were restricted. The *Lex* granted to those in *libertate* (*see* note to **9**(b) above) something of the status of *Latini Coloniarii*. They were known as *Latini Juniani* (Junian Latins). They were not allowed to vote or to make a will.

> NOTE
>   (i) Junian Latins could become citizens in a number of ways, *e.g.* by *anniculi probatio* (*see* (iv) above); by service in the Watch; by building a ship and importing corn; if a woman, by having three children.
>   (ii) Justinian granted citizenship to all Junian Latins.

11. Other methods.

(a) *By Redemption*. A newly-born child sold as a slave (*see* **7**(h) above) could be redeemed.

(b) *Pardoned servi poenae* (*see* **7**(d) above) regained freedom.

(c) *By jus postliminii* (*see* note to **6** above) a returned captive might recover his freedom.

(d) *By returned price*, in the case of a freeman who had become enslaved as the result of allowing himself to be sold fraudulently as a slave (*see* **7**(g) above).

(e) *A pagan's slave* who was converted to Christianity was given his freedom.

(f) *As a reward for important services*, e.g. under *Sc. Silanianum* (c. A.D. 10) for the discovery by a slave of his master's murderer. Constantine enacted that liberty should be given to slaves who procured the conviction of coiners of bad money.

(g) *By Edict of Claudius* (*see* **8**(c) above).

> NOTE: Until the time of Justinian a slave owned by two or more masters could not be freed except by agreement of all the masters.

12. Status of the freedman. A freedman owed certain duties to his patron:

(a) *Operae* (*work*). The freedman had to promise on oath to perform services for his patron. An *actio operarum* could be used to enforce this promise (*see* XVI, **36**).

(b) *Obsequium* (*deference*). A freedman had to respect his patron and had a duty to support him in case of need. He could not sue his patron without the Praetor's consent.

(c) *Jura in bonis*. A patron had the right to succeed to a freedman who was childless and intestate. In the case of a childless, but testate, freedman he succeeded to one-half of his property. (Justinian allowed one-third of the property in this case, and nothing if the freedman's goods were less than 100 *aurei* in value) (*see* also XIII, **33**(a) and XIV, **17**).

> NOTE
> (i) A freedman was allowed to achieve the status of a free-born man by an Imperial act of grace (*restitutio natalium*), but this required his patron's consent.
> (ii) A slave who had been freed because of his master's misconduct owed no duties to him.

QUASI-SERVILITY

13. Its meaning. The Institutes speak of men as being either free or slaves. In fact, some persons enjoyed a status which was between freedom and slavery.

(a) *The colonus*—a settler on a large estate. He was the tenant of a landowner, but was not allowed to leave the land. He was sold with the land and could not be ejected from it.

(b) *The hired gladiator*—a freeman who had contracted to serve as a gladiator.

(c) *The cliens*—one who enjoyed the protection of a patron.

(d) *The Servus Publicus Populi Romani* (*see* note to **4** above).

(e) *The bona fide serviens*—a freeman who, as the result of an error, was serving as a slave.

(f) *The debitor addictus*—a debtor who had been handed over to his creditor for sale (*see* XV, **17**).

(g) *The redemptus*—a slave captured in battle who had bought his liberty by paying a ransom.

(h) *The statuliber*—a slave who had been freed by will subject to a condition.

> EXAMPLE: Stichus, slave of Marcus, is to be manumitted according to the following direction in the will of Marcus: "Let Stichus be free when Titius dies." Until Titius dies Stichus becomes the property of Marcus's heir, who can sell him. Stichus will become free, nevertheless, on the death of Titius.

(i) *The person in mancipio* (*mancipium* = civil bondage). *Mancipium* existed where a *paterfamilias* conveyed someone in his power to another by mancipation, *e.g.* where a *paterfamilias* made noxal surrender of a son (*see* XX, **7**).

> NOTE:
> (i) A person manumitted from civil bondage became *sui juris*, because mancipation extinguished *potestas*.
> (ii) Mancipation had become obsolete by Justinian's time and was formally abolished by him.

PROGRESS TEST 8

1. Explain the terms (a) *ingenuus*, (b) *libertinus*. **(2)**
2. Was the Roman slave considered to be a person or a *res*? **(1)**
3. Had the slave any property rights? **(3)**

4. Who were (a) *Servi Publici Populi Romani*, (b) *Dediticii*? **(4, 7)**

5. "Without legal status, he was subject to the unrestrained whims of his owner." Consider this comment on the position of a slave in the time of Hadrian. **(8)**

6. What was the legal status of a child born to a slave mother? **(6)**

7. Explain how enslavement could arise as the result of capture in time of war. **(6)**

8. What was *jus postliminii*? **(6)**

9. Compare the position of a slave and a child in *potestas* in the early law. **(3, 4)**

10. " Ingratitude displayed by a freedman to a patron could bring most serious consequences." Comment. **(7, 12)**

11. What was the effect of (a) *Lex Cornelia de Sicariis*, (b) *Lex Petronia*? **(8)**

12. Explain manumission *per vindictam*. **(9)**

13. Outline the provisions of *Lex Aelia Sentia*. **(10)**

14. What were the duties of a freedman towards his patron? **(12)**

15. Explain (a) *restitutio natalium*, (b) *statuliber*. **(12, 13)**

16. Give four examples of the status known as "quasi-servility". **(13)**

PART THREE

THE LAW OF PROPERTY

CHAPTER IX

THE DIVISION OF THINGS

THE MEANING OF A "THING"

1. The Law of Property. The Roman Law of Property was concerned essentially with things, their acquisition and their transfer.

2. Res (things). The Romans considered as *res* objects, and rights in objects, which had economic value. *Res* could be:

(a) *Res corporales* (*see* **3** below), or
(b) *Res incorporales* (*see* **4** below).

3. Res Corporales (physical things), *i.e.* tangible objects, such as a chair, a slave, a barn, a plot of land.

4. Res Incorporales (non-physical things), *i.e.* a right to which an economic value attaches, as, for example, the right of Flavius to pasture his cattle on land belonging to Marcus (*see* XI, **8**), or the right to inherit another's property.

Division of Things according to Gaius

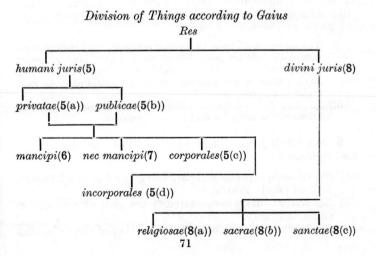

5. Res humani juris. These were *res*, the ownership of which was vested in human beings. They might be:

- (a) *Res privatae*—things in private ownership, or
- (b) *Res publicae*—things in public ownership, *e.g.* an aqueduct.

All such *res* were either:

- (c) *Res corporales* (see **3** above), or
- (d) *Res incorporales* (*see* **4** above),

and were also either:

- (e) *Res mancipi* (*see* **6** below), or
- (f) *Res nec mancipi* (*see* **7** below).

6. Res mancipi. This name referred to those things capable of being transferred only by the mode of transfer known as *mancipatio* (*see* X, **12**). Such things were: houses and lands in Italy; rustic servitudes over Italian lands (*see* XI, **8**(*a*)); slaves; animals such as the horse and the ox.

NOTE: The mode of transfer known as *in jure cessio* (*see* X, **13**) was sometimes employed for the transfer of *res mancipi*.

7. Res nec mancipi. These were things which could be conveyed by a mode other than *mancipatio*, *e.g.* public lands; wild animals such as elephants; agricultural implements.

NOTE
- (i) The grouping of these particular *res* under the heading of *res mancipi* might be the result of their having been regarded as the real wealth of an agricultural community, or their having been taken into account in an assessment for purposes of the census.
- (ii) In A.D. 531 Justinian abolished the formal distinction between *res mancipi* and *res nec mancipi*.

8. Res divini juris. These were *res* "in divine ownership" and comprised:

- (a) *Res religiosae:* things dedicated to gods of the underworld, such as family graves;
- (b) *Res sacrae:* things consecrated to the gods above, such as altars, temples;
- (c) *Res sanctae:* things under the protection of the gods, such

as the walls of a city, the violation of which was a capital offence. Legend had it that Romulus, founder of Rome, killed Remus, his brother, for leaping the city walls.

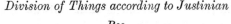

Division of Things according to Justinian

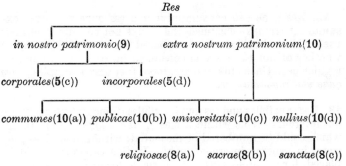

9. In nostro patrimonio. Things vested in private ownership.

10. Extra nostrum patrimonium. Things not owned privately, comprising:

(a) *Res communes:* those things open to everyone, *e.g.* the sea.
(b) *Res publicae:* those things owned by the state, *e.g.* a harbour.
(c) *Res universitatis:* those things owned by a corporate body or municipality, *e.g.* a theatre.
(d) *Res nullius.* Justinian included under this heading *res religiosae, sacrae* and *sanctae.* The phrase *res nullius* was also applied to:

    (i) things which, in general, could not be privately owned;
    (ii) things which could be owned, but which, at a particular moment, had no owner, *e.g.* a wild animal; an island formed in the sea; things discovered on the seashore; things discovered after intentional abandonment by their owners; treasure trove (*thesaurus*). The finder of treasure (except that buried for safe-keeping) was entitled to one-half, the other half going to the person who owned the land on which the treasure was found (*see* also X, 6).

OTHER CLASSIFICATIONS

11. Res mobiles and res immobiles (movable and immovable things). Land, for example, was in the category of *res immobiles*. (During the period of the classical law land fell into two categories: *solum provinciale* and *solum italicum*. By the time of Justinian there was no longer such a distinction.)

12. Res quae usu consumuntur and res quae non usu consumuntur (things consumed and things not consumed in their use). This classification was based on a consideration of whether or not the *res* was consumed in, or worn out by, its regular use. Garments, money, food, fuel were examples of *res quae usu consumuntur*.

13. Res fungibiles and res non fungibiles (things which are or are not interchangeable within a class). *Res fungibiles* were things which could be numbered or measured; within their class they were, in general, interchangeable. In this category would be placed, for example, corn, oil. A slave, for example, would be considered as an individual unit and would be classified in the category of *res non fungibiles*.

NOTE
   (i) A further classification is mentioned in the Digest (*see* III, 13)—*res quae sine interitu dividi non possunt* (things which could not be divided without a diminution of their value), for example, a painting, a slave.
   (ii) Intangible rights such as *patria potestas* (*see* V) or freedom were not considered to belong to the category of *res incorporales* (*see* **4** above).

PROGRESS TEST 9

1. With what was the Roman Law of Property concerned? (**1**)
2. What was a *res*? (**2**)
3. Explain the following terms: (a) *res incorporales*, (b) *res privatae*. (**4, 5**)
4. Outline the Division of Things, according to Gaius. (**5–8**)
5. Give examples of (a) *res mancipi*, (b) *res sanctae*. (**6, 8**)
6. What was the Division of Things, according to Justinian? (**9, 10**)

7. What were the meanings of the phrase '*res nullius*'? (**10**)

8. Under which headings, at the time of Justinian, would the following *res* have fallen:

(a) a harbour, (b) a municipal amphitheatre, (c) a privately-owned team of horses? (**9, 10**)

9. Explain (a) *res quae usu consumuntur*, (b) *res fungibiles*. **12, 13**)

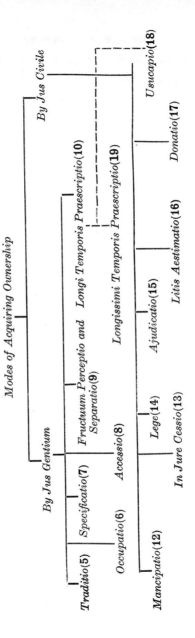

Modes of Acquiring Ownership

By Jus Gentium

By Jus Civile

Tradilio(**5**)

Occupatio(**6**)

Specificatio(**7**)

Accessio(**8**)

Fructuum Perceptio and Separatio(**9**)

Longi Temporis Praescriptio(**10**)

Longissimi Temporis Praescriptio(**19**)

Mancipatio(**12**)

In Jure Cessio(**13**)

Lege(**14**)

Ajudicatio(**15**)

Litis Aestimatio(**16**)

Donatio(**17**)

Usucapio(**18**)

CHAPTER X

OWNERSHIP AND ITS ACQUISITION

OWNERSHIP AND POSSESSION

1. Essential difference. The owner of property may not always be in possession of it.

EXAMPLE: Balbus owns a horse which is stolen by Pindarus. After the theft Pindarus has possession of the horse, but the ownership remains vested in Balbus.

Conversely, one may have legal possession of property, while another has its ownership.

EXAMPLE: Maevius occupies a farm as the tenant of Seius. Seius has the ownership, Maevius is in possession.

To have mere physical control in possession was described as *detentio*, or *naturalis possessio*. Mere *detentio* conferred no rights on the possessor. Where *detentio* was accompanied by *animus possidendi* (*i.e.* the intention to deal with the property as though one owned it), this was referred to as *possessio*, or *civilis possessio*. *Possessio* was often protected by Praetorian Interdicts (*see* XXIII, **13**).

2. Quiritary ownership. (Dominium ex jure Quiritium). The term "quiritary" was possibly derived from Quirinus, the name bestowed, after his apotheosis, on Romulus. Romans were known at one time as *Populus Romanus Quirites*. Under *jus civile*, only quiritary ownership was recognised as conferring *dominium* (*i.e.* full ownership). It was available only to those who possessed Roman citizenship.

3. Bonitary ownership (*bona* = possessions).
(a) A person might have received *res mancipi* (*see* IX, **6**) by *traditio* (*see* **5** below) instead of having received them by the formal method of *mancipatio* (*see* **12** below). In such a case he did not obtain quiritary ownership (*see* **2** above). An informal acquisition of ownership effected in this and some

77

other modes was protected by the Praetor. Thus, where A had transferred *res mancipi* to B by *traditio*, instead of by *mancipatio*, and A had then attempted to recover the *res* by an action, the Praetor allowed B to plead, against A, the *exceptio rei venditae et traditae* (*see* XXII, 23). This directed the judge to absolve B if the thing had been sold and delivered to him by A. The ownership thus acquired by B was known as bonitary ownership. Ownership by *occupatio* (*see* 6 below) of abandoned things usually conferred bonitary ownership.

(b) The *actio Publiciana* (introduced by the Praetor Publius, *c.* 66 B.C.) was available in the following cases:

    (i) To assist a bonitary owner. In the example above, B could acquire *dominium* by usucaption (*i.e.* possession over a period of time) (*see* 18 below). If B's period of occupation was then interrupted he was allowed to bring the *actio Publiciana* on the fictitious ground that his period of usucaption was complete.

    (ii) To assist a *bona fide* possessor. If X purchases from Y, in good faith, *res mancipi* or *res nec mancipi*, and Y is not the real owner, X has no action if the real owner evicts him. In such a case X can bring an action against Y. Should X be disturbed in his possession by any other person he can bring the *actio Publiciana* and will succeed if his title is prior to defendant's and derived from the same source.

        NOTE: Justinian ended the distinction between bonitary and quiritary ownership.

OWNERSHIP UNDER JUS GENTIUM

4. Modes of acquiring ownership. Under *jus gentium* (*see* II, 8) ownership could be acquired in the following ways:

    (a) *Traditio* (*see* 5 below)
    (b) *Occupatio* (*see* 6 below)
    (c) *Specificatio* (*see* 7 below)
    (d) *Accessio* (*see* 8 below)
    (e) *Fructuum Perceptio* and *Separatio* (*see* 9 below)
    (f) *Longi Temporis Praescriptio* (*see* 10 below)

5. Traditio (Delivery).

(a) *Its meaning.* A transfer of possession from A to B, with the intention of transferring ownership, resulting in the vesting of ownership in B.

(b) *Necessary conditions:*
  (i) The property transferred must be *res nec mancipi* (*see* IX, **7**).
  (ii) A must have the intention to transfer ownership to B, and B must have the intention to receive it.
  (iii) A must be competent to transfer, and B to acquire, in this mode.
  (iv) The property must be capable of delivery and of acquisition by delivery.
  (v) The property must be transferred by the owner or his authorised agent.
  (vi) Transfer must be by physical or constructive delivery. Constructive delivery could be: *traditio brevi manu* (delivery with the short hand), where a transferee had possession but not ownership of the property, *e.g.* Brutus has borrowed a plough from Gaius and Gaius then gives it to him; *traditio longa manu* (delivery with the long hand), where property is placed in sight of the transferee who is told to take it; symbolic delivery, *e.g.* by delivering the keys to a granary, so that the transferee acquires possession of the grain; *constitutum possessorium* (agreement to possess), *e.g.* Seius owns a plough and keeps possession of it while agreeing to its ownership being vested in Marcus.

  NOTE
  (i) Because *traditio* was informal it could be carried out by a representative of the owner.
  (ii) In the case of a contract of sale, delivery did not transfer ownership until the price had been paid.

6. Occupatio (occupation).

(a) *Its meaning.* To seize a *res nullius* (*see* IX, **10**(d)) with the intention of dealing with it as one's own property.
(b) *Things captured from the enemy.* These generally became the property of the captors, with the exception of immovables, which were taken by the State.
(c) *Animals ferae naturae (naturally wild).* Wild birds and beasts, for example, became the property of the taker and remained his for as long as they were under his control.

  EXAMPLE: Lucius enters on Casca's land without permission and takes a wild bird. The bird was considered to belong to Lucius.

(d) *Animals mansuetae naturae (naturally tame)*. These animals were creatures which, although naturally wild, had been tamed and had the *animus revertendi* (habit of going away and returning). Whilst the *animus revertendi* continued they remained the property of their owner.

(e) *Precious stones found on the seashore*. These belonged to the finder.

(f) *Unoccupied islands in the sea*. In the rare event of an island 'springing up' in the sea, its ownership vested in the first occupant.

> NOTE: Under Hadrian, a finder of abandoned treasure-trove (*thesaurus*) took an equal share with the land owner. But in the event of his having entered on the land with the deliberate intention of looking for treasure, treasure so found belonged entirely to the land owner.

7. Specificatio (specification).

(a) *Its meaning*. The creation from another's material of a thing "of a new kind" (*nova species*), *e.g.* a seat made from wood, or bronze transformed into an ornament.

(b) *Ownership of the new article*. The answer of the Proculians (*see* II, **19**): the creator of the new article. The answer of the Sabinians: the owner of the material. Justinian's solution: if the article was not reducible to its original form it belonged to the maker, but if it was reducible it belonged to the owner of the material; if any part of the material belonged to the maker the *nova species* belonged to him.

> EXAMPLE: Pindarus uses gold belonging to Aulus in order to fashion a goblet. In a dispute as to possession of the goblet, in the time of Justinian, since the goblet can be reduced to its original form it would belong to Aulus, who would have to compensate Pindarus for his work.

8. Accessio (accession).

(a) *Its meaning*. An occurrence in which things under different ownership combine physically and cannot be separated or restored to their original condition, as, for example, where a portion of Titinius's field is swept away by a river in flood and becomes attached to a river bank belonging to Publius.

(b) *Alluvio* (*earth deposited by water*). Where silt is deposited on the banks of a river, the owner of the banks becomes owner of the deposit.

(c) *Plantatio* (*planting*) *and satio* (*sowing*). Brutus's seed, scattered on Lucius's field, belongs to Brutus until it takes root in Lucius's land.

(d) *Natural increment*. He who owned the female parent generally owned its offspring.

(e) *Commixtio and Confusio* (*mixing of solids and liquids*). Where the solids can be separated with ease (e.g. a flock of sheep) there is no resultant common ownership; where this is not possible (*e.g.* where X's grain is mixed with Y's grain) there is common ownership of the mixture.

(f) *Inaedificatio* (*building*). The general rule was that anything built on the soil belonged to it. Where A built on B's land, the general rule was that the owner of the principal (B) owned the accessory (the building). By a legal fiction the owner of materials remained their owner and could demand their return on the building's being demolished. Hence, rules for compensation were evolved. They were:

  (i) Where A built, *bona fide*, on A's land with B's material, B could bring an *actio in factum* for the value of the materials used, or an action for the materials on the destruction of the building.

  (ii) Where A built *mala fide* on A's land with B's materials, B could bring the *actio de tigno injuncto*, or the *actio ad exhibendum*, or the *actio furti* (*see* XIX, **13**) if the materials had been stolen from him, or he could claim the materials when the building was demolished.

  (iii) Where A built on B's land with A's materials, if A was in possession of the land and acted *bona fide* he could claim compensation from B. If A was not in possession and acted *bona fide* he could claim the materials on destruction of the building.

(g) *Islands emerging in river beds*. Where an island emerged in the middle of a river it belonged to the riparian owners in proportion to the length of the river banks they owned.

(h) *Avulsio*. Where A's land was swept away by a river and combined with B's, the land belonged to B as soon as any trees on A's land took root on B's soil.

D

(i) *Scriptura.* X writes verses on parchment belonging to Y. The whole belongs to Y. Where Y makes a claim to the parchment and refuses to pay X, X can raise in a subsequent action the *exceptio doli* (*see* XXII, 23).

(j) *Pictura.* Where P paints on Q's tablets, the tablets were held to be accessory to the painting and P was considered to be their owner.

9. Fructuum Perceptio and Separatio (Perception and Separation of Fruits).

(a) *Its meaning.* The right to acquire the fruits of land.

(b) *What was included.* The produce of fields and gardens under cultivation; the offspring of animals; rents from property.

10. Longi Temporis Praescriptio (Prescription over a long period of time).

(a) *Its meaning.* By retaining provincial land and some movables for an uninterrupted period of ten years (where owner and possessor lived in the same municipality or, under Justinian, in the same province) or twenty years in other cases, the possessor could acquire ownership.

(b) *Necessary conditions.* There must be *possessio*, not merely *detentio* (*see* 1 above); the land had to be capable of being alienated; the persons concerned must have *commercium* (the right to hold property and to make contracts); there must be just title (*see* also *Uscapio* 18 below, and *Longissimi Temporis Praescriptio*, 19 below).

OWNERSHIP UNDER JUS CIVILE

11. Modes of acquiring ownership. Under *jus civile* ownership could be acquired in the following ways:

(a) *Mancipatio* (*see* 12 below)
(b) *In Jure Cessio* (*see* 13 below)
(c) *Lege* (*see* 14 below)
(d) *Adjudicatio* (*see* 15 below)
(e) *Litis Aestimatio* (*see* 16 below)
(f) *Donatio* (*see* 17 below)
(g) *Usucapio* (*see* 18 below)

12. Mancipatio (mancipation).

(a) *Its meaning.* Mancipation was a fictitious sale. Assume
that Brutus is acquiring property by mancipation from
Trebonius. In the presence of five Roman citizens and a
libripens, who holds the bronze balance, Brutus grasps the
property and declares, "This thing I state to be mine by
quiritary right and has been bought by me with this bronze
piece and bronze balance." Brutus strikes the balance with
a piece of bronze which is given to Trebonius as the price.

(b) *Its use.* Only *res mancipi* (*see* IX, **6**) could be conveyed by
mancipation. Note its use in *testamentum per aes et libram*
(*see* XII, **11**), emancipatio (*see* V, **12**) and in *adoptio* (*see*
V, **8**).

NOTE
   (i) Where the property to be transferred was immovable,
     only its symbolic presence at the place of sale was
     required.
  (ii) In time, the ceremony of mancipation disappeared, hav-
     ing given way to the transfer of ownership by *traditio*
     (*see* **5** above).

13. In Jure Cessio (cession before the court).

(a) *Its meaning.* *In jure cessio* was a transfer involving the
fiction of vindication. Assume that Brutus wishes to acquire property from Trebonius in this mode. Brutus, in the
presence of a magistrate, grasps the property and says,
"This thing, I state, is mine, *ex jure Quiritium*." The
magistrate asks Trebonius whether he wishes to state a
counter-claim. Trebonius says, "No," or remains silent.
The magistrate then awards the property to Brutus. Of
this mode of transfer it has been said, "The owner cedes,
the cessionary vindicates, the magistrate awards."

(b) *Its use.* The transfer of corporeal property, both *res mancipi* and *res nec mancipi*, could be effected in this mode.
Usufructs and praedial servitudes (*see* XI, **8** and **9**(a))
could be created and extinguished by this method.

NOTE
   (i) The effective acquisition of property in this manner
     was possible only if the property was capable of ac-
     quisition *ex jure Quiritium*.
  (ii) *Mancipatio* and *in jure cessio* had disappeared by the
     time of Justinian.

14. Lege (by statute).

(a) *Its meaning.* The vesting of property in a person by title derived from a *lex*.

(b) *Example.* Constitution of Valentinian and Theodosius (*see* XIX, **19**).

15. Adjudicatio (by judicial award).

(a) *Its meaning.* In actions for the division of property (*judicia divisoria*) the judge could divide the property among the parties.

(b) *Examples. Actio communi dividundo*—an action for the division of property held in common; *actio finium regundorum*—an action for deciding boundaries.

16. Litis Aestimatio (estimate of liability in a matter in issue).

A judge, in an action for the restoration of property, could order the possessor to restore it to the plaintiff. Plaintiff might then estimate its value and defendant might be allowed to keep the property on payment of its value.

17. Donatio (by gift).

(a) *Types of Gift. Donationes mortis causa* (*see* XIII, 29) and *Donationes inter vivos.*

(b) *Donationes inter vivos* (*gifts between living persons*). Under Justinian gifts over 500 *solidi* (200 *solidi* under Constantine) required registration. A donor who was sued on his promise could plead the *beneficium competentiae* if there was a possibility of the gift preventing payment of his creditors. *Donationes* could be revoked where the donee had displayed considerable ingratitude to the donor. Under Justinian a gift to a freedman was revocable only where the donor had been childless when the gift was made and where, subsequently, children had been born to him.

18. Usucapio (acquisition of ownership by long use).

(a) *Its meaning.* Under certain circumstances it was possible for a Roman citizen to acquire ownership of property, or be confirmed in a defective title, by lapse of time.

(b) *Necessary conditions.* The property must have been acquired legally; the possessor must have had *commercium* (*see* **10**(b) above) and must have been in actual possession; the property had to be capable of being alienated.

(c) *Period of usucapio.* By the XII Tables, two years for land and one year for other things. Any interruption of this period (*usurpatio*), *e.g.* by forcible ejection, extinguished a previous period of possession. An heir to property could add the uninterrupted period of possession of the previous holder to his own period of possession. Should a possessor lose possession before the period of usucapion had ended, the Praetor could allow him an *actio Publiciana in rem*; this permitted him to recover as though the period had ended.

19. Reforms of Justinian. In A.D. 528–531, Justinian reformed and merged *usucapio* and *longi temporis praescriptio.* The term *usucapio* was used only in connection with the acquisition of movables; the period was to be 3 years. The term *longi temporis praescriptio* was limited to the acquisition of immovables; the period was to be 10 or 20 years (*see* **10**(a) above). *Longissimi Temporis Praescriptio* (prescription by the longest period of time): a bona fide possessor who lacked a just title and who had held the property for 30 years could vindicate such property from the owner. It was essential, however, that the property should have been obtained without violence. Actions by the original owner were barred after 30 years (following an enactment of Theodosius).

OWNERSHIP ACQUIRED THROUGH AN AGENT

20. Ownership acquired through slaves. Where a slave received property in circumstances which would have given him full ownership had he been a freeman, the ownership of such property was acquired by the master.

21. Ownership acquired through free persons acting as agents. A *paterfamilias,* for example, could acquire ownership through those in his *potestas* (*see* V, **3**).

22. Ownership acquired through a procurator. A *procurator* was an agent employed to manage his principal's property.

Any property of which he acquired the ownership in his capacity as *procurator* passed into his employer's ownership.

NOTE: In the case of joint ownership, co-owners were entitled to the produce of their property in proportion to their shares. Upon the death of a co-owner his share passed to his heir. Co-owners had to share in any losses caused by animals or slaves held in common, and a co-owner had to defray expenses incurred by other co-owners on behalf of the property. The *actio communi dividundo* could be brought by joint owners who wished their property to be divided.

PROGRESS TEST 10

1. What was the distinction in Roman Law between ownership and possession? (1)

2. Who has possession and who has ownership in the following cases:

(a) Publius lets his house to Trebonius?

(b) Casca seizes Aulus's purse and runs off with it? (1)

3. What was meant by *Dominium ex jure Quiritium*? (2)

4. Explain the nature of bonitary ownership. (3)

5. Enumerate the modes of acquiring ownership under *jus gentium*. (4)

6. Define (a) *traditio*, (b) *traditio longa manu*. (5)

7. Outline the legal principles involved in the ownership of animals which were (a) *mansuetae naturae*, (b) *ferae naturae*. (6)

8. In A.D. 120, Flavius hears that abandoned treasure might be under some rocks on land belonging to Messala. A year later he enters Messala's land and, after searching for the treasure, discovers it under the rocks. Comment. (6)

9. How did the Sabinians answer the problem involved in *specificatio*? What was Justinian's solution? (7)

10. Define and illustrate *accessio*. (8)

11. Explain the principles involved in the following case: Cassius writes a poem on a parchment belonging to Brutus. Cassius then claims the parchment. (8)

12. What was meant by *longi temporis praescriptio*? (10)

13. What were the modes of acquiring ownership under *jus civile*? (11)

14. Explain *in jure cessio*. (13)

15. How could ownership be acquired by *adjudicatio*? (15)

16. What were the necessary conditions for the acquisition of ownership by *usucapio*? (18)

17. Could ownership be acquired through a slave? (20)

18. What was meant by *longissimi temporis praescriptio?* **(19)**

19. Explain (a) *donationes inter vivos,* (b) perception and separation of fruits. **(9, 17)**

20. Under what circumstances was the *actio Publiciana* available to assist a *bona fide* possessor? **(3)**

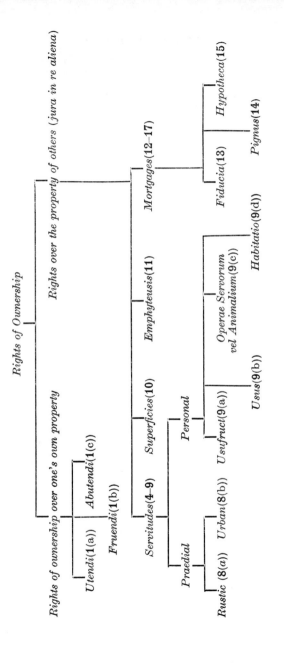

CHAPTER XI

PROPERTY RIGHTS

RIGHTS OF OWNERSHIP AND THE RIGHT TO ALIENATE

1. The rights of ownership. *Dominium* (full ownership) gave the owner three important rights:

(a) *jus utendi*—the right to use the property;
(b) *jus fruendi*—the right to enjoy the fruits and profits of the property;
(c) *jus abutendi*—the right to consume or destroy the property.

Rights such as these were known as real rights (rights *in rem*) because the owner could assert these rights "against the world," whereas personal rights (rights *in personam*) could be asserted only against another person.

> EXAMPLE: Caius employs Publius to build a house. The agreement between them gives Caius a right *in personam* against Publius. On the completion of the house, Caius, its owner, acquires rights *in rem* concerning the property, which can be asserted "against the world."

2. The right to alienate. Certain persons were deprived of the right to alienate their property freely, *e.g.*

(a) Under Justinian, husbands could not dispose of dotal immovables (*see* VI, **26**(c)(iii)).
(b) Lunatics and spendthrifts had restricted rights of alienation (*see* VII, **3**–**4**).
(c) A *pupillus* could not alienate without his tutor's consent (*see* VII, **5**).

RIGHTS OVER THE PROPERTY OF ANOTHER

3. Jura in re aliena (rights over another's property). In some cases a person owned property, but his rights over such property might be limited.

EXAMPLES

(i) Veratius owns grazing land on which Lucius has a right to pasture his cattle (*see* **8**(a) below).
(ii) Veratius owns land over which Lucius has the right to walk and ride (*see* **8**(a) below).

In both of these cases Veratius's rights of enjoyment of his land are limited by Lucius's rights. The most important *jura in re aliena* were:

(a) *Servitudes* (*see* **4** below)
(b) *Superficies* (*see* **10** below)
(c) *Emphyteusis* (*see* **11** below)
(d) *Mortgages* (*see* **12** below)

SERVITUDES

4. Their meaning and nature. A servitude was said to exist where X possessed rights *in rem* over the property of Y. In the following cases, for example, the property of Titinius is encumbered with servitudes in favour of Cassius:

(i) Where Cassius enjoys the right of drawing water from a fountain on Titinius's land;
(ii) Where Cassius enjoys the right of sailing on Titinius's lake;
(iii) Where Cassius enjoys a right to the labour of Titinius's slave.

Servitudes might be praedial (*see* **8** below) or personal (*see* **9** below) and praedial servitudes could be rustic (*jura praediorum rusticorum*) or urban (*jura praediorum urbanorum*) (*see* **8**(a) and (b) below).

Servitudes were either:

(a) Affirmative (*jus faciendi*), whereby the owner of the servient tenement was obliged to allow the performance of certain acts by the owner of the dominant tenement.
(b) Negative (*jus prohibendi*), whereby the owner of the servient tenement was obliged to refrain from performing certain acts, *e.g.* increasing the height of his house.

5. Rules applicable to servitudes.

(a) *Vicinitas.* Dominant and servient tenements had to be close to each other.
(b) *Perpetua causa.* The exercise of the servitude, in the case of land, had to be possible in perpetuity.

(c) *Utilitas*. Use of the servient tenement had to be of advantage to the dominant tenement.

(d) *Indivisibility*. A servitude had to be indivisible. Where the dominant tenement was partitioned the servitude remained applicable to all the parts. Where the servient tenement was partitioned it was possible to confine the incidence of the servitude to certain parts.

(e) *Non-transferability*. Servitudes were not, in general, transferable.

(f) *Nulli res sua servit*. (No one may have a servitude over his own property.) If, for example, in **4**(i) above Cassius should acquire the ownership of Titinius's land, the existing servitude would merge in the ownership. Should Cassius, at a later date, sell this land the servitude would not revive automatically.

(g) *Servitus servitutis esse non potest*. (There cannot be a servitude of a servitude.) Assume that Ligarius has the right of leading water (*see* **8**(a)(iii) below) through a pipe which passes over the land of Marcus and Decius. Ligarius might agree to allow Marcus and Decius to draw water from the pipe, but such an agreement could not operate as a servitude.

(h) *Servitus in faciendo consistere non potest*. (A servitude cannot consist of doing.) *See* **4**(a) and (b) above. The owner of the servient land is obliged to allow an act or to refrain from performing an act.

(i) *Servitus civiliter exercanda est*. A servitude must be so used as to cause as little inconvenience as possible.

6. The creation of servitudes. Servitudes could be created in the following ways:

(a) *Mancipatio* (*see* X, **12**), for the creation of a rustic servitude in Italic land.

(b) *In jure cessio* (*see* X, **13**), for the creation of urban servitudes.

NOTE: (a) and (b) were obsolete by the time of Justinian.

(c) *Adjudicatio*. By judicial decision, *e.g.* in partition actions where a judge could award a servitude over property.

(d) *Deductio* (*by reservation*). Where, for example, a person alienates property with the reservation that it shall be servient to property retained by him.

(e) *Testamento (by will)*. Where, for example, X instructs his heir to allow Y the exercise of a right over property.

(f) *Usucapio (see* X, **18**). *Lex Scribonia* (in the reign of Tiberius) forbade this method of creating servitudes.

(g) *Longi Temporis Praescriptio (see* X, **10**). The period was, under Justinian, 10 years *inter praesentes*, and 20 years *inter absentes*.

(h) *Lege (by statute)*. See, for example, the creation of a usufruct in an emancipated son's property *(see* V, **4**(d)).

(i) *Pacts and Stipulations (see* XVI and XVIII).

(j) *Traditio et Patienta*. A type of informal contract by which X acquiesced in the exercise of an apparent servitude over his property by his neighbour, Y.

7. The extinction of servitudes. Servitudes could be extinguished in the following ways:

(a) *Destruction or complete change of the property*, so that usefulness of the servient property ceased.

(b) *Non-utendo (non-user)*. 2 years for praedial servitudes *(see* **8** below); 10 or 20 years under Justinian.

(c) *Confusio (merger)*. This occurred where the ownership of dominant and servient tenements vested in one person.

(d) *Remissio (surrender)*. By *in jure cessio* or by simple agreement.

(e) *Expiration of time*. Where, for example, the servitude had been granted for a stated number of years.

(f) *Death*. A usufruct *(see* **9**(a) below) ends with the death of its possessor.

8. Praedial Servitudes *(praedium* = a plot of land). Praedial servitudes were rights over immovables. These rights were exerted by the owner of a *praedium dominans* (dominant tenement) over a *praedium serviens* (servient tenement). Such servitudes were of two types: rural, or rustic *(servitutes praediorum rusticorum)* and urban *(servitutes praediorum urbanorum)*.

(a) *Rural (or rustic) servitudes*. These were generally rights over land:

    (i) *Rights of way*, e.g. *iter* (right to pass), *actus* (right to drive a carriage or animal), *via* (right to walk and drive), *jus navigandi* (right of sailing over a permanent lake).

(ii) *Rights of pasture*, e.g. *jus pascendi* (right to put cattle to graze on another man's land).

(iii) *Rights to water*, e.g. *aquae ductus* (leading water in pipes, or in stone channels; such a right could be granted for summer only, in which case it was known as *aquae aestiva*); *aquae haustus* (drawing water from a well or fountain); *pecoris ad aquam apulsus* (watering one's cattle on another's land).

(iv) *Miscellaneous rural servitudes*, e.g. *jus lapidis eximendae* (right of quarrying stones); *jus arenae fodiendae* (right of digging sand).

(b) *Urban servitudes*. These were generally rights over things erected on land, e.g. *oneris ferendi* (right to support for a building), *tigni immittendi* (right to drive a timber beam into a neighbour's wall), *altius non tollendi* (right to prevent a neighbour increasing the height of his house), *stillicidi recipiendi* (right to discharge rain water on to a neighbour's property), *ne luminibus officiatur* (right to light), *jus projiciendi* (right to space above a neighbour's land, e.g. a projecting balcony), *cloacae mittendae* (right to pass a sewer below a neighbour's ground), *latrinae sive sterculini* (right to have a dung heap against a neighbour's wall).

9. Personal Servitudes. Praedial servitudes were held by virtue of the ownership of a house or land; personal servitudes did not depend on such ownership. The most important personal servitudes were: *ususfructus, usus, operae servorum vel animalium, habitatio.*

(a) *Ususfructus.*

(i) *Definition.* A right to use and enjoy the fruits of another's property, provided that its substance remained unimpaired.

(ii) *Property in which a usufruct might be held.* In general the property had to be *res quae non usu consumuntur* (*see* IX, **12**), e.g. land, or a slave. A *senatusconsultum* in the time of Tiberius allowed a quasi-usufruct to be created in *res quae usu consumuntur*, such as corn.

(iii) *Its duration.* In the absence of an agreement that it should last for a specified number of years it lasted for the life of the *ususfructuarius.*

(iv) *Security.* The *ususfructuarius* had to give security (*cautio ususfructuaria*) to the owner, promising a restoration of the property when the usufruct ended.

(v) *Protection of the usufruct.* By *vindicatio ususfructus.*

(vi) *Rights of the usufructuary.* Use and enjoyment of the fruits (but note that ownership in fruits passed to the usufructuary only when gathered); use of stock and implements of a farm; right to lop pollards; right to open mines; right to fish and hunt; right to the offspring, milk, hair, wool of animals.

(vii) *Duties of the usufructuary.* Not to alter the character of a building, *e.g.* not to change it from a house into a shop; not to use a slave other than for work in which he had been trained; to deal with the property as would a *paterfamilias, i.e.* with great care; to carry out repairs; to pay any taxes on the land.

(viii) Creation of a usufruct. In the modes indicated at 6(b)(d)(e)(h)(i) above.

(ix) Termination of a usufruct. By 7(b)(c)(d)(e)(f) above.

NOTE: Where a usufruct existed in the case of a female slave, the *ususfructarius* was entitled to the fruits of her work, but not to her children.

(b) *Usus (use).*

(i) *Definition.* A usufruct, but without the right to take the fruits, and limited to the personal wants of the *usuarius* and his family.

(ii) *Rights of the usuarius.* He had only the use of property, *e.g.* he could use a house only for his occupation, but could not let it; he could take only those things necessary for his daily use; he could not alienate the property; he could use the labour of a slave in person only.

(iii) *Duties of the usuarius.* He had to share with the owner the expense of repairs to the property; he could not modify the character of the property.

(c) *Operae servorum vel animalium (right to the services of slaves or animals belonging to another).* Unlike a usufruct, this right was not lost by *non-utendo* (non-use).

(d) *Habitatio (habitation).* The right to use the house of another.

OTHER JURA IN RE ALIENA

10. Superficies (= a building attached to the soil).

(a) *Definition.* A right to the enjoyment, in perpetuity or for a long period, of a building upon the land of another.

(b) *Rights of the superficiarius.* He could use the building and could alienate or pledge it. He had no rights over the land and paid a ground rent (*solarium*).

11. Emphyteusis

(a) *Definition.* A grant of full rights of ownership over the land of another in perpetuity or for a long period subject to forfeiture under particular circumstances (*see* (e) below) and subject to the payment of a yearly rent.

(b) *Origin.* Lands taken from the State's enemies were leased by the State in perpetuity or for long periods; these lands were known as *agri vectigali* (*vectigal* = rent). By the time of the Empire tenants had rights *in rem* over such leases, which were given the Greek name of *emphyteusis*.

(c) *Was the emphyteuta a purchaser or hirer of the land?* This question was settled by the Emperor Zeno who considered the *jus emphyteuticarium* to be neither ownership nor lease; it was held to be governed by its own special type of contract.

(d) *Rights and duties of the emphyteuta.* He had to pay the annual rent, failing which he could be ejected (after 3 years non-payment under Justinian); he had to cultivate the land; he had to manage the property so that its value did not fall; he had to pay any taxes on the land and deliver the receipts to the owner; he could use and enjoy the land and its fruits and could alienate or pass the *emphyteusis* to his heirs; he could modify the character of the land provided that he did not damage it.

(e) *Forfeiture.* On non-payment of rent; on proof that the property had been allowed to deteriorate; on an irregular attempt to transfer the *emphyteusis*, *e.g.* without giving notice of sale.

NOTE
  (i) If the *emphyteuta* wished to sell the property he had to obtain the owner's consent, which could be given subject to an indemnification of 2% of the purchase price. The owner could also pre-empt, but had to state his intention to buy within 2 months.
  (ii) Where, in an attempt to cause a forfeiture, the owner refused to accept the rent, the *emphyteuta* could, in the presence of a witness, deposit the money in a sealed container. This was held to be an effective tender of payment.

12. Mortgages. Security for a debt owed by X to Y might be personal or real. The real mortgage took the form of Y's being granted rights over X's property. The Roman mortgage developed in three forms: the first form was *fiducia*, the second was *pignus*, the third was *hypotheca*. These are considered in turn below.

13. Mancipatio cum fiducia (fiducia = trust). The debtor (mortgagor) transferred by *mancipatio* (*see* X, **12**) the ownership and possession of *res mancipi* (*see* IX, **6**) to the creditor (mortgagee). Ownership and possession had to be reconveyed to the mortgagor on repayment of the debt. The mortgagor was protected by the *actio fiduciae*; the mortgagee had the counter-action *contraria actio fiduciae*.

14. Pignus (pledge). Transfer of possession, but not ownership, of *res mancipi* or *res nec mancipi*, by the mortgagor to the mortgagee. The mode of transfer was *traditio* (*see* X, **5**). On payment of principal and interest the property had to be delivered up to the debtor. At the time of Justinian the mortgagee could sell the property after three notices and a delay of two years. Should he have been unable to sell the property he was allowed to present a petition to the Emperor requesting ownership of the property. Where the petition was granted the mortgagor was given another two years before foreclosure. The mortgagor had an *actio in factum* (later replaced by the *actio pigneraticia*) to enforce reconveyance of possession (*see* also XVI, **17–20**).

15. Hypotheca (= mortgage). This was a Praetorian mode of mortgage under which the mortgagor passed neither ownership nor possession of the mortgaged property, but agreed to hold certain things as security for the debt. An *actio Serviana*, under which a landlord was given agricultural implements and stock as a security for his tenant's rents, was extended so that it secured the rights of any mortgagee.

16. Tacita hypotheca (mortgages by operation of law). These charges over property were implied by law and did not arise out of agreement. Examples were:
(a) The *Fiscus* (Treasury) had a charge on a debtor's property for his taxes.

(b) Legatees had a charge over a testator's estate for payment of legacies.

(c) Wives had a charge for return of the *dos* (*see* VI, 26(c)).

(d) Bankers had charges on land bought with money they had lent.

(e) *Pupilli* had a charge over property bought with their money by tutors.

> NOTE: A rural hypothec existed in favour of a landlord over his tenant's crops; an urban hypothec existed in favour of a landlord over his tenant's furniture.

17. Successive Mortgages. Assume that Brutus owns land worth 4,000 *aurei*. He gives a hypothec on it for debts of 2,000 *aurei* to Cassius and, later, a further hypothec for a debt of 500 *aurei* to Publius and for 1,000 *aurei* to Trebonius. Provided that the value of Brutus's property did not fall below 3,500 *aurei*, Cassius, Publius and Trebonius would have adequate security. If the value of the property fell to 2,500 *aurei*, who would receive payment? The principle adopted was (as in English Law) *qui prior est tempore potior est jure* (he who is first in time has the strongest claim in law). Hence, Cassius and Publius would be paid. The application of this principle took second place, however, to the demands of the *Fiscus* for debts arising from taxes and to a wife suing for the return of *dos*. Other examples of hypothecs enjoying privilege are noted in **16** above.

PROGRESS TEST 11

1. What were the general rights of ownership? **(1)**

2. Explain the difference between rights *in personam* and rights *in rem*. **(1)**

3. Were there any circumstances in which owners were prevented from alienating their property? **(2)**

4. What was meant by the phrase *jura in re aliena*? **(3)**

5. Explain the nature of a servitude. What was the difference between affirmative and negative servitudes? **(4)**

6. "Servitudes did not arise in the absence of *vicinitas* and *perpetua causa.*" Discuss. **(5)**

7. Explain (a) *servitus in faciendo consistere non potest*, (b) *servitus servitutis esse non potest*. **(5)**

8. State seven ways in which a servitude could be created. **(6)**

9. What was the effect on a servitude of *non-utendo*? **(7)**

10. Give examples of urban and rural servitudes. **(8)**

11. Define usufruct. What were the rights of a usufructuary? **(9)**

12. Outline the rights of the *usuarius*. **(9)**

13. Explain (a) *superficies*, (b) *solarium*. **(10)**

14. What was *emphyteusis*? Under what circumstances could the *emphyteuta* sell the property? **(11)**

15. Brutus, the *emphyteuta*, attempts to pay his rent to Casca, the landlord. Casca wishes to cause a forfeiture and he refuses to accept payment. What course of action is open to Brutus? **(11)**

16. Explain *mancipatio cum fiducia*. **(13)**

17. Define *pignus*. **(14)**

18. Give examples of the *tacit hypothec*. **(16)**

PART FOUR

THE LAW OF WILLS AND SUCCESSION

CHAPTER XII

THE NATURE AND FORMALITIES OF SUCCESSION

THE NATURE OF SUCCESSION

1. Testate and Intestate Succession.

(a) *Where a deceased person left a will (testamentum)* and succession took place according to the terms of that will the succession was said to be testate.

(b) *Where the deceased person did not leave a will* succession was said to be intestate (*see* also XIV, **1**).

(c) *Testate succession could not co-exist with intestate succession* with regard to a particular estate.

> EXAMPLE: By his will, Titius fails to dispose of his entire estate. His testamentary heirs are Brutus and Maevius. The undisposed part of the estate goes, not to Titius's heirs on intestacy, but to Brutus and Maevius in proportion to their shares in the inheritance.

2. The importance of the heir.
The most important function of a Roman will was the nomination of an heir; the distribution of the estate in accordance with the will was a secondary matter. Where a will failed to nominate an heir it was of no worth. The possibility of dying without an heir, and the attendant possibilities of extinction of the family unit, were viewed with great concern. The soul of the deceased required its funeral rites, and family worship required a head to conduct the ceremonies. Hence, the nomination of an heir who would be responsible for these duties, and in whom the *persona* of the deceased was thought to continue was very important.

3. Successio in universum jus.
The heir succeeds to the *hereditas* which involves legal representation of the deceased. He succeeds, therefore, to the *universitas juris, i.e.* the entirety of the deceased man's duties and rights. Hence, the heir

101

enjoyed the benefits of the rights and discharged the responsibilities of the duties.

NOTE: The entire legal personality of the deceased did not pass to the heir. Thus, for example, where the deceased had held public office this office did not pass to his heir.

VALIDITY OF A WILL

4. General. So that a will might be effective it was essential:

(a) that it be valid *ab initio* (from the beginning);
(b) that it remain valid until the heirs enter upon their inheritance;
(c) that the heirs enter.

5. Validity ab initio. There were five requisites for validity *ab initio*:

(a) The will had to be made in a certain form;
(b) An heir, or heirs, had to be appointed properly;
(c) Certain persons had to be appointed as heirs or disinherited;
(d) Certain persons had to be provided for;
(e) Capacity to make a will (*testamenti factio*) was required in the case of parties to the will.

6. Observance of forms. Proper form was essential. A variety of forms existed and are considered in **11–17** below.

7. Proper appointment of the heir. This was a vital part of the will (*see* **2** above) and is considered in XIII.

8. Appointment or disherison. The will was void unless certain persons were instituted as heirs or disinherited in express terms. This disherison might be of a class or of an individual (see XIII, **17–18**).

9. Provision for certain persons. In certain cases, where a will disinherited, without good cause, children or parents, or possibly brothers and sisters, it was void.

10. Testamenti factio. There had to be competency on the part of the testator, witnesses to the will and the heir(s) (*see* **18–21** below).

NOTE: A will might fail even though all the above requirements had been met, *e.g.* the heir might refuse to accept.

TYPES OF WILL AND FORMAL REQUIREMENTS

11. Early types of will.

(a) *Testamentum in Comitiis Calatis* (*will made before the Comitia Calata*). The *Comitia Calata* was the name given to the *Comitia Curiata* (see I, **7**(a)) when it met twice a year for the purpose of hearing oral declarations. The will was declared orally before the assembly and could be made probably by patricians only.

(b) *Testamentum in procinctu* (*will made on the eve of battle. Procinctus = army ready for action*). Since the army was the *Comitia* in arms this type of will differed little from that considered in (a) above. It could be made orally in the presence of a group of three or four comrades-in-arms and might consist merely of a nomination of heirs.

> NOTE: (a) and (b) above had become obsolete during the final period of the Republic.

(c) *Testamentum per aes et libram* (*will made with bronze and balance*). This rested on the formalities of *mancipatio* (*see* X, **12**). The testator, in the presence of five witnesses and a *libripens* (balance-holder), wrote out his will, usually on wax tablets, and formally conveyed his family to another person (*familiae emptor*). This conveyance was subject to a trust which allowed the testator a life interest in his estate. As an alternative mode the testator made an oral declaration of his will and did not commit it to written form. In the later law a testator was allowed to seal the tablets on which his will was written; their contents were not disclosed at the ceremony. Such a will had to be in Latin; in A.D. 439 it was enacted that Greek could be used.

12. The Praetorian will. So that injustice might not result from a failure to observe the forms in **11**(c) above, the Praetor could intervene where necessary and recognise a written will sealed in the presence of witnesses. In such a case the Praetor could give the heirs *bonorum possessio secundum tabulas* (*see* XIII, **33**).

13. The Tripartite will. This type of will was introduced in the later Empire by Theodosius and Valentinian. It had three sources:

(a) *Jus civile:* witnesses were required at the making of a will;
(b) *Praetorian Edict:* the seals of seven witnesses were required;
(c) *Imperial Constitutions:* the testator's signature was required.

> NOTE: In the time of Justinian it was enacted that the entire transaction of making a will should be without interruption (*uno contextu*) and separate from any other business.

14. The private nuncupative will (testamentum per nuncupationem. Nuncupatio = the pronouncing of a vow). An oral will made without formalities was valid if made in the presence of seven witnesses.

15. The public nuncupative will (testamentum apud acta conditum). This involved an oral declaration in the presence of a magistrate. The declaration was entered in the official records.

16. The public written will (testamentum principi oblatum). The written will was formally delivered to the Emperor with a request that it be confirmed.

> NOTE: In Justinian's time the general methods of making a will were **13–16** above.

17. Special types of will.

(a) *Wills of those unable to read.* Five witnesses sufficed. It was essential that they knew the names of those to be instituted as heirs.
(b) *Wills of the blind.* Seven witnesses and a notary, or the town secretary, were required. The blind testator was obliged to recite the names and shares of the heirs and the details of any legacies.
(c) *Wills of those suffering from a contagious disease in time of epidemic.* Seven witnesses were required, but it was not necessary for them to be present at one time.
(d) *Wills made in rural areas (testamentum ruri conditum).* Because of the difficulty of finding witnesses, five sufficed.

(e) *Wills of parents* (*testamentum parentum*). An informal will by which a parent disposed of his estate among his children could be construed as a *fideicommissum*, or trust (*see* XIII, 32). If written out by the testator no witnesses were needed. Where such a will provided for persons other than the testator's children it was enacted by Theodosius and Valentinian that such a provision was to be considered void and the property was to go to the testator's children.

(f) *Wills of soldiers*. A privilege was accorded by Julius Caesar to soldiers on active service and, later, to seamen, whereby those on active service could make a written or oral will without any formalities. The privilege lasted during the soldier's or sailor's active service and for one year following his retirement. (This type of will was not the same as one made *in procinctu*.)

TESTAMENTI FACTIO

18. Its meaning. *Testamenti factio* meant the capacity to make a will, to take a benefit under a will, or to witness a will. Without *testamenti factio* a will could be void.

19. Testamenti factio activa. A testator had to have the right to make a will at the time of his making it and also at the time of his death. His capacity to make a will had to exist at the time the will was made. With some exceptions, all Roman citizens had the capacity to make a will. There was no such capacity in the case of:

(a) A *prodigus* (spendthrift).
(b) *Deaf, dumb, blind people*, except in special cases (*see* **17** above).
(c) *Impubes*.
(d) *Captives*. The will of a returned captive made prior to his captivity was held valid on his return (*see jus postliminii*, VIII, 6(b)).
(e) *Those who had lost their freedom or their citizenship*, e.g. slaves (except the *Servi Publici Populi Romani*, who could leave half their *peculium* by will (*see* note to VIII, 4)), and Junian Latins.
(f) *Those who could not be owners*, e.g. those not *sui juris* (except, *e.g.* males in *potestas* who could make a testa-

mentary disposition of *peculium castrense* and *quasi-cas-trense* (*see* V, **4**)).

(g) *Dediticii* (*see* VIII, 7(i)).

(h) *Those who had not the right to alienate property*, e.g. lunatics.

(i) *Those incapacitated as a penalty*, e.g. publishers of libels, apostates.

(j) *Those whose status was uncertain* (*de statu suo incerti*), e.g. a son in power who was not sure whether his *paterfamilias* was dead.

> NOTE: In the early law women had no testamentary capa-city. By the time of Hadrian they had this capacity and, if under tutelage (*see* VII, **11**), could make a will without *auctoritas tutoris*.

20. Testamenti factio passiva.

(a) An heir had to have capacity to take at "three moments":

  (i) at the time the will was made,
  (ii) at the time of the testator's death,
  (iii) at the time of his entry upon the inheritance.

A change in the heir's status between (i) and (ii) had no consequence if restored in time, but a change in status be-tween (ii) and (iii) prevented an heir from entering. A legatee also required capacity at the "three moments."

(b) There was no capacity to take (*jus capiendi ex testamento*), either as heir or as legatee in the following cases:

  (i) *Incertae personae* (uncertain persons, e.g. a corporation, or a person who was nominated with insufficient precision).
  (ii) *Peregrini* who did not possess *commercium* (the right to hold property and make contracts).
  (iii) *Women, under Lex Voconia* (c. 168 B.C.), could not be made heirs to persons enrolled in the first class of the census. This did not affect women as legatees and the restriction became obsolete when the census disappeared.
  (iv) *Heretics*.
  (v) *The children of those declared to be traitors*.
  (vi) *Latin Junians* were prohibited by *Lex Junia* (*see* VIII, **10**(c)) from taking under a will, unless they acquired citizenship within 100 days of the date at which they could have accepted the inheritance.
  (vii) *Lex Papia Poppaea* (*see* VI, **12**–**13**) prohibited the child-less and unmarried from taking more than one half of

an inheritance. The inheritance thus lost was declared vacant (*caducum*) and passed to married persons who had children and who had benefited under the will. In their absence the inheritance went to the *Fiscus*. Justinian abolished *caduca*.

21 Testamenti factio relativa. A witness had to possess capacity at the time he witnessed the will. The following were disqualified: women; *impubes*; slaves; deaf and dumb; lunatics; those convicted of bribing magistrates; those who were members of the testator's *familia*; those in the heir's family.

NOTE: A legatee was a competent witness to a will.

OPENING AND INTERPRETATION OF A WILL

22. Opening of a will. All, or most of the witnesses, were obliged to attend the opening of a will. They acknowledged the seals, after which the will was opened and read in public, in the Basilica or the Forum, in the magistrate's presence. It was then copied and the original placed in the public archives. To open a will in any other manner brought liability for a penalty of 5,000 *sesterces* (*see* also **24**(j) below). Inspection of wills was not allowed if there was any uncertainty as to whether or not the testator was dead.

23. Interpretation of a will. Erasures could be considered as signs of an intention to revoke. Extrinsic evidence was not admitted to prove the meaning of illegible writing. The testator's language had to be construed in its ordinary sense. Where the literal sense of a will conflicted with the testator's known intention, the intention prevailed.

INVALIDATION OF A WILL

24. A will was invalidated in the following ways:

(a) Lack of *testamenti factio* in the parties:
(b) Refusal of heirs to accept (in this case the will was considered as abandoned—*destitutum*):
(c) Death of the heir(s) before the testator:
(d) Testator or heir suffering *capitis deminutio* (*see* IV, **6**); in such a case the will was described as *irritum*—made in vain, or inoperative:

(e) Success of a *querela inofficiosi testamenti* (*see* XIII, **21**):

(f) Intentional destruction of a will:

(g) Revocation resulting from the testator having made a second will:

(h) Lapse of time. If a will was not renewed after ten years it lapsed:

(i) By the appearance of a new *suus heres* (*see* XIII, **4**) of the testator, *e.g.* by adoption, or by the birth of a child to the testator after the making of a will in which the child has been neither instituted nor disinherited. Such a will was said to be *ruptum*—broken. *Lex Junia Velleia* (A.D. 10) allowed a testator to disinherit or institute as heir:

(i) a person conceived before the will was made and who might be born as the testator's *suus heres* in his lifetime;

(ii) a grandchild born before the date of the will who, as a result of his father's death, might become *suus heres* in the lifetime of the testator.

(j) In post-classical times, by the intentional opening of the will in an unofficial manner.

PROGRESS TEST 12

1. Explain what was meant by testate and intestate succession. (**1**)

2. Why was the nomination of an heir of importance to the Romans? (**2**)

3. What was meant by succession to *universitas juris*? (**3**)

4. State the pre-requisites of a will valid *ab initio*. (**5**)

5. Explain *testamentum per aes et libram*. (**11**)

6. What was the *testamentum apud acta conditum*? (**15**)

7. Trebonius, old and blind, wishes to make a will. What formalities were needed? (**17**)

8. What privileges in the making of wills were accorded to soldiers? (**17**)

9. Explain *testamenti factio*. (**18**)

10. Could a woman under tutelage make a valid will? (**19**)

11. "An heir required capacity at three vital moments." Discuss. (**20**)

12. Were the following considered to be competent witnesses to a will: (a) a child aged 11, (b) legatees under the will? (**21**)

13. Outline the formalities of opening a will. (**22**)

14. When was a will said to be (a) *destitutum*, (b) *ruptum*? (**24**)

CHAPTER XIII

HEIRS AND THE INHERITANCE

FORMAL APPOINTMENT

1. Institutio Heredum (appointment of heirs). This was the real object of a will (*see* XII, 2). The words of appointment had to be placed after the clauses of disherison (*see* **17** below). A legacy placed before the words of appointment was void (but this restriction was abolished by Justinian). After A.D. 339 no form of words would invalidate an appointment provided that the testator's intention was clear.

> NOTE: Where there were no legacies and no disherison, it was possible for a will to consist of a few words, *e.g. "Caius mihi heres esto."* ("Be Caius my heir.")

2. Limiting conditions. The appointment of an heir could not be made subject to a limitation of time. The rule was: *semel heres semper heres* (once an heir always an heir).

TYPES OF HEIR

3. Heres necessarius (necessary heir). This was a slave of the testator who, by the will, was made free, was appointed heir and was obliged to accept the inheritance. He was allowed a *beneficium separationis* (right of separation) by the Praetor, under which he could apply to keep separate from the inheritance anything he acquired after the testator's death. The appointment of such an heir took place when the estate was insolvent, or near-insolvent, so that subsequent proceedings were in his name and posthumous ignominy was not brought on the master's name.

4. Heres suus et necessarius (family and necessary heir). A *heres suus* was a descendant of the testator, in his power, and likely to become *sui juris* on the testator's death, or a child or a further descendant who might be born posthumously. Such a family heir could not reject the inheritance. Where he had not intermeddled with the estate the Praetor allowed him a *beneficium abstinendi* (right to abstain), under which his property was rendered not liable for satisfaction of the estate's liabilities.

5. Heres extraneus (heir outside the testator's power). The nomination of such a person was construed as a mere offer of the inheritance, which was without legal effect until accepted. Such an heir was given a time limit (*cretio—see* **12** below) in which to accept or reject the inheritance. Later, the Praetor allowed a *spatium deliberandi* (*see* **12**(b) below) and Justinian allowed, as an alternative, *beneficium inventarii* (*see* **12**(c) below). Once an acceptance or refusal had been signified it could not be withdrawn.

SUBSTITUTION OF HEIRS

6. Substitutio vulgaris (common substitution). Should an heir not accept the inheritance, the will would fail. So that this might be avoided a testator could substitute an heir. A form of such substitution was, "Let Cominius be my heir. If Cominius shall not be heir, let Maevius be heir." *Substitutio vulgaris* took effect only where the heir did not take the inheritance.

NOTE: Several substitutes could be named in the place of one heir, or one as a substitute for several heirs.

7. Substitutio pupillaris (substitution for children). This type of substitution could be made by a *paterfamilias*. Pupillary substitution could not be postponed beyond puberty and was not possible in the case of an emancipated child. The procedure was:

(a) The *paterfamilias* appointed as his heir a child in his power;
(b) A substitute was appointed in the possible event of the child's failing to become heir, for example, by dying before the testator or before reaching the age of puberty.

8. Substitutio exemplaris (exemplary substitution). Justinian allowed a testator with descendants who were insane to substitute others for them. The substitutes had to be descendants of the insane person, or a brother or sister, or their descendants. The substitution endured only for the period of insanity.

CO-HEIRS

9. Division of the inheritance. It was possible for a testator to arrange for the division of his estate among several co-heirs. In such a case the estate was treated as a unit, and where the shares of some co-heirs were not specified they took (in equal proportions) the difference between the shares assigned by the will and a unit of twelve. Where the assigned shares were greater than twelve, they took (in equal proportions) the difference between that sum and the next multiple of twelve.

EXAMPLE: Flavius leaves a will under which Publius is heir to three parts of the estate, Maevius is heir to seven parts, Lucius to eight parts. Titius and Lepidus are made co-heirs, but their shares are not stated. The appropriate calculation would be as follows: Sum of shares assigned by the will = 3 + 7 + 8 = 18. 24 (next multiple of 12) less 18 = 6.
Titius and Lepidus take 6/2 shares each, *i.e.* 3 shares each.

VESTING OF THE INHERITANCE

10. In the heres necessarius. No acceptance was necessary and the estate vested in the *heres necessarius* on the death of the testator.

11. In the heres suus et necessarius. The Praetor allowed the *heres* a *beneficium abstinendi* (a right to abstain), but this was lost if the *heres* had interfered with the estate in any way. The estate's creditors could apply to the Praetor for the imposition on the *heres suus* of *tempus ad deliberandum* (a fixed time for deliberation) and, at the end of this fixed time, the *beneficium* was not allowed if the *heres* had not come to a decision.

12. In the heres extraneus.

(a) Entry on the inheritance (*aditio hereditatis*) was necessary and could take place by a formal declaration, or informally by actions which manifested an intention to enter. A period of 100 days (*cretio vulgaris*) was allowed the *heres* in which to make his decision. This period began when he became aware of his rights. He might be allowed, alternatively, *cretio continua*, calculated from the date of testator's death.

(b) *Cretio* became obsolete and the Praetor then allowed the *heres* a *spatium deliberandi* (time in which a decision could be made) of not more than 100 days, but this time could be extended by the Praetor in cases of emergency. The *heres* was allowed to inspect the accounts of the estate during this period.

(c) Justinian introduced (A.D. 531) the *beneficium inventarii* (benefit of inventory) by which the heir was saved from liability for the estate's debts, over and above his own assets, if he began an inventory of the estate's assets within 30 days of being made aware of his rights and if he completed the inventory within a further 60 days.

FORFEITURE OF THE INHERITANCE

13. Forfeiture as a punishment. In certain cases the estate was forfeited to the Exchequer as a punishment inflicted on the heir. Examples of such cases were:

(a) Where a testator declared in writing that he considered an heir to be unworthy and that he should be deprived of the inheritance.

(b) Where an official in a province married a woman of that province during his term of office, he could be deprived of any property she left to him.

(c) Where an heir had been guilty of serious misconduct towards the testator, *e.g.* as when the testator had died through the negligence or fault of the heir, or when the heir had refused to carry out the injunctions in a will, or when the heir had concealed or destroyed the will.

LIABILITY FOR DEBTS

14. The general rule. The heir was obliged to pay all the debts of the deceased and his liability was unlimited. Where there were several heirs and the debts were divisible, the debts could be allocated in proportion to the shares.

15. Protection of creditors. An insolvent heir who had entered into a solvent estate could be asked by the creditors for security. Failure to provide security could lead to proceedings in insolvency being brought by the Praetor against the heir. An alternative form of protection was *separatio bonorum*, by which the creditors applied (within 5 years of acceptance by the heir) for an order to treat the testator's property as separate from the heir's. The result of this was that creditors of the deceased were given the right to be paid in full before creditors of the heir.

16. Priority of payments to creditors. Under Justinian the order of payment in the case of an insolvent estate, of which an inventory had been made, was:

(a) Funeral expenses;
(b) Expenses of registering the will;
(c) Expenses of winding up the affairs of deceased and making an inventory;
(d) Creditors secured by mortgage;
(e) Other creditors whose claims had been presented.

DISHERISON

17. The general rule. In order that a will might be valid it was necessary to nominate certain persons as heirs or to disinherit them expressly. The rule possibly reflected the Roman idea of co-partnership in the family property. During the life of the *paterfamilias* the children were considered as co-owners of the property, and on his death they were considered as possessing administrative powers over that property. Hence, unless they were removed from such a position by disinheritance, no stranger could be nominated as heir.

18. Operation of the rule.

(a) The *sui heredes* had to be instituted or disinherited; they could neither be passed over nor omitted.
(b) Hence it was necessary to disinherit *nominatim* (by name) at the time the will was made. The correct form was: "*Cassius filius meus exheres esto.*" ("Be my son Cassius disinherited.")
(c) Other *sui heredes, e.g.* daughters and grandchildren, had to be disinherited, but in such a case specific mention of

E

names was not necessary—a general clause sufficed, *e.g.* *"Ceteri omnes exheredes sunto."* ("Be all the rest disinherited.")

(d) Disherison *nominatim* was necessary in the case of *postumi* (children born after the making of a will), or adopted children.

19. Praetorian extension of the rule. The Praetors changed the disinherison rule so that it included all those descendants admitted as *unde liberi* to intestate succession (*see* XIV, **11**). This involved the disherison of all males *nominatim* and females *inter caeteros*. In the absence of this they could be given *bonorum possessio contra tabulas* (see **33** below) (*see* also *Lex Junia Velleia*, XII, **24**(i)).

20. The rule under Justinian. Disherison *inter caeteros* was abolished, but all those disinherited had to be mentioned by name.

     NOTE: The will of a soldier on active service provided an exception to the general rules of disherison. The omission in such a will of any reference to children had the effect of their disherison *nominatim*.

QUERELA INOFFICIOSI TESTAMENTI

21. Its meaning. A *querela inofficiosi testamenti* (plaint of the unduteous will) was an action which could be brought by certain relations of the deceased on the grounds that the will had not provided for them. The defendant was the testamentary heir, and the *querela* had to be brought against him within 5 years of his entering upon the inheritance. The action did not pass to the heirs of the plaintiff(s).

22. The action.

(a) *Descendants of the testator*, ascendants, and brothers and sisters (in a case where, for example, "base persons" (*turpes personae*) such as those of a low social status, had been preferred to them) could bring the action.

(b) *The action originally grew out of the fiction* that the testator was insane at the time of making the will which was, therefore, invalid.

(c) *Plaintiff was required to show that* he had not been disinherited with good reason and that he had not received
an equitable portion of the estate. This statutory portion
(*legitima portio*) was fixed at one-quarter of what plaintiff
would have received on intestacy.

(d) *Since the querela was an action of last resort* it was not available to those who had other means of challenging the will.
Nor was it available to those who had taken a benefit
under the will.

(e) *The result of a successful querela* was the invalidation of the
will.

> NOTE: A successful *querela* could be instituted where an
> estate had increased in value after the making of the will
> and where, as a result, the plaintiff had not received a fair
> share. This could be prevented by the insertion of a clause
> by which a share considered to be inadequate could be refer-
> red to the arbitration and decision of a fair-minded man.

23. Justinian's reforms.

(a) *A querela could be brought only where* the plaintiff had received nothing under the will. An inadequate portion, however, could be increased to the statutory amount by the
actio ad supplendam legitimam.

(b) *After A.D. 536 a testator with up to four children* was obliged
to leave them at least one-third of his estate in equal
shares. A testator with more than four children had to
leave them at least one half in equal shares.

(c) *After A.D. 542 a testator had to institute as heir* those of his
descendants who were entitled to succeed him on an
intestacy.

(d) *Legal grounds for disherison were enumerated.* Some of
them were as follows:

  (i) Grounds for disinheriting one's child: assaulting or seri-
  ously injuring the parent; adultery with the father's
  wife; neglecting to redeem a parent from captivity;
  neglecting to look after an insane parent; frustrating a
  parent's attempt to make a will; heterodoxy of the child.

  (ii) Grounds for disinheriting one's parent: accusing the child
  of a serious crime (except treason); attempts on the
  child's life; neglecting an insane child.

  (iii) Grounds for disinheriting one's brother and sister: attempts on the testator's life; accusing the testator of a

capital offence; attempting to deprive the testator of his property.

NOTE: A *querela inofficiosae donationis* could be brought where the testator decreased the value of portions to his heirs by excessive gifts *inter vivos*.

LEGACIES

24. General. A legacy (*legatum*) could be a *res corporalis* or *res incorporalis*. The creation and transfer of legacies were based on strict rules.

25. Types of legacy. (*See table opposite*).

NOTE
- (i) A legacy could fail in the following cases: where the property was destroyed; where the legatee predeceased the testator; where the will was invalid; where the testator revoked the legacy either formally (by a subsequent will) or informally (by removal of the legacy from the will) (*see* also *Lex Falcidia*, **28**(c) below).
- (ii) Where a legacy was intended for a creditor of the deceased it was presumed to be in satisfaction of the debt, except where the legacy was in excess of the debt.

26. Sc. Neronianum (*c.* A.D. 54). This *senatusconsultum* allowed a legacy expressed in a form which was inappropriate (*minus aptis verbis*) to take effect as if expressed in the most favourable form. For example, a legacy which was void because it was expressed, say, *per vindicationem* would be construed as having been expressed *per damnationem*, if valid in that form.

27. Acquiring the legacy. Generally the legatee obtained an expectancy (which was transmissible to his heirs) on the opening of the will. Justinian substituted for this date the time of the testator's death. This expectancy was referred to as *dies cedit* ("the day is on its way"). When the heir entered upon the inheritance the legacy could be claimed at once—*dies venit* ("the day has come").

NOTE: The legatee could not take away without authorisation the *res* left to him.

Type of Legacy	Formula needed for its creation	Ownership of the res	Property the testator could give	Actions available
(a) *Legatum per vindicationem* (legacy by giving a claim to some thing)	"*Do lego.*" ("I give and bequeath.")	Passed at once to legatee	Only that which belonged to him by Quiritary title (*see* X, 2)	*Rei vindicatio*
(b) *Legatum per damnationem* (legacy by condemning heir to pay)	"*Dare damnas esto*" ("Let my heir be condemned to give.")	Had to be transferred by heir to legatee	His own property, or that which was not yet in existence ("next year's crops") or that which belonged to another; in such a case the heir was obliged to purchase it or compensate the legatee with its value	*Actio ex testamento*
(c) *Legatum per Praeceptionem* (legacy by allowing legatee to take in advance)	"*Praecipito.*" ("Let the legatee take in advance.")	Vested at once in the legatee	Only his own property	*Actio familiae erciscundae*
(d) *Legatum sinendi modi* (legacy by way of sufferance)	"*Damnas esto sinere . . .*" ("Let my heir be condemned to allow the legatee to take.")	Had to be transferred by heir to legatee	Only his own property	*Actio ex testamento*

28. Legislation which restricted the amount of legacies. By
the XII Tables a testator had unrestricted freedom as to the
amount of legacies. The result was that in many cases, legacies
were so excessive that little was left for the heir on whom fell
full liability for the estate's debts. Consequently many heirs
refused to enter. Three legislative measures (the first two of
which were unsuccessful) attempted to remedy this.

(a) *Lex Furia* (*c.* 204 B.C.). Except in the case of a blood
relation no legatee could accept a legacy of more than one
thousand *asses*, on penalty of paying four times the excess.

(b) *Lex Voconia* (168 B.C.). No legatee could receive more than
the heir. This applied only to the wills of those enrolled
in the first class of the census.

(c) *Lex Falcidia* (40 B.C.). Legacies could not exceed three
quarters of the inheritance. The heir had to receive at
least one quarter of the estate (*Quarta Falcidia*). The
estate's value, for the purposes of this *Lex*, was its value
at the testator's death less debts, funeral expenses and the
value of any slaves manumitted in accordance with the
will. The testator could expressly exclude the operation of
this *Lex*. The *Lex* did not apply to soldiers' wills. Justinian did not allow the benefit of the *Lex* to an heir who
claimed *spatium deliberandi* (*see* **12**(b) above).

29. Donationes mortis causa (gifts in contemplation of death).
No will was needed to make these gifts. It was essential that
they were not to take effect until the donor's death and, until
that time, they were revocable. Revocation by will was also
possible. *Testamenti factio* (*see* XII, **18**) was not required from
either donor or donee. In A.D. 530 Justinian enacted that five
witnesses to a gift were required and that a gift made in these
circumstances did not require registration. If the donor survived the donee the gift did not take effect.

CODICILS AND TRUSTS

30. The significance of Codicils. Codicils (*codicilli* = little
books) were informal directions, written or oral, to an heir.
When used in addition to a will, they were read as part of the
will; in the absence of a will they were considered as directions
binding on the heir *ab intestato*. A codicil made before a will

had to be ratified in the will; an anticipatory clause was usually inserted in the will to cover codicils made after the will. Justinian required five witnesses to a codicil.

31. Clausula codicillaris (codicillary clause). The addition of this clause to a will allowed that will, in the event of its failure, to be construed as a series of codicils binding on the heir *ab intestato*.

NOTE
   (i) The Roman codicil should not be confused with the codicil in English Law, which is an instrument added to a previously-made will.
  (ii) A person could not be properly disinherited by codicil.
 (iii) Legacies given by a codicil had to be confirmed in the will.
 (iv) A person who could not make a will could not generally make a codicil.

32. Trusts (fideicommissa). The trust came into existence as a method of circumventing prohibitions on certain classes of people becoming heirs or receiving legacies (*see* XII, 20). Under Augustus trusts became legally binding. From the time of Claudius they were enforced by the *Praetor Fideicommissarius*.

(a) *Their form.* They could be declared in a codicil or will, or by an informal oral statement.
(b) *Their pattern.* Property was given initially to the *fiduciarius, i.e.* the trustee, who was obliged to hand it to the *fideicommissarius*. The property could consist of an entire estate or a single *res*.
(c) *Their use for family settlements.* It was possible for A to give B, his heir, land under the condition that it was to be preserved and transferred to C, B's eldest son, who was to preserve it in trust for his eldest son, D. Perpetuities were prevented by a declaration of Justinian that property could not be tied up in this way for more than four generations (*Nov.* 159).
(d) *Their revocation.* An informal revocation was possible and its effect was to extinguish the trust completely.
(e) *Their development.*

      (i) In the early stages an heir who was compelled to hand over property to another person, by trust, remained liable for any debts attached to the inheritance. He could stipulate with the *fideicommissarius* for an indemnity against claims by creditors of the estate.

(ii) By the *Sc. Trebellianum* (A.D. 57) a creditor was allowed to sue the *fideicommissarius* directly.

(iii) By the *Sc. Pegasianum* (A.D. 70) an heir was forbidden to refuse to make entry. He was allowed, however, to retain one quarter of the inheritance (*Quarta Pegasiana*) but was liable for all the estate's debts.

(iv) Under Justinian the heir was obliged to make a formal entry. He could retain one quarter of the inheritance, and the liabilities attached to the estate were divided between the heir and the *fideicommissarius* in proportion to their shares.

> NOTE: A trust could not be created by a person who lacked the capacity to make a will.

BONORUM POSSESSIO

33. Bonorum Possessio (possession of goods). By Praetorian Edict, succession could be granted by the Praetor in cases where he considered the claimant to be entitled equitably. The title thus granted did not confer on the successful claimant the status of heir (*see* XXIII, **16**). *Bonorum possessio* could be *contra tabulas* or *secundum tabulas*.

(a) *Contra tabulas* (*in opposition to the will*). Under *jus civile* an emancipated son could not claim his father's inheritance. But where he was omitted from his father's will or not disinherited in express terms (*see* **17–20** above), the Praetor was able to give him *bonorum possessio* under the condition that he brought into hotchpot with his brothers in *potestas* all his property held at the time of his father's death (*collatio bonorum*). *Bonorum possessio contra tabulas* could also be given to a patron who had been left less than half of his freedman's estate (*see* VIII, **12**(c) and XIV, **17**).

(b) *Secundum tabulas* (*in accordance with the will*). Where a will lacked validity under the civil law, *e.g.* because of failure to observe all the formalities, the Praetor was able to give effect to it. A grant *secundum tabulas* was made only where a testator had possessed *testamenti factio* at the time of his death, where the persons instituted under the will had the capacity to succeed under the civil law, and where no claim had been made against the will. (For *bonorum possessio intestati see* XIV, **9–14**).

PROGRESS TEST 13

1. *"Titius mihi heres esto."* Could these words create a will? **(1)**
2. Explain the phrase *"semel heres semper heres."* **(2)**
3. What was involved in *substitutio pupillaris*? **(7)**
4. Explain (a) *beneficium abstinendi*, (b) *cretio vulgaris*. **(11, 12)**
5. What was the effect of Justinian's introduction of the *beneficium inventarii*? **(12)**
6. Marullus dies as the direct result of the negligence of his heir, Ligarius. Could the inheritance be forfeited in these circumstances? **(13)**
7. What was the general rule concerning the heir's liability for the testator's debts? **(14)**
8. Explain *separatio bonorum*. **(15)**
9. What was disherison? **(17)**
10. How were the rules of disherison changed under Justinian? **(20)**
11. Under what circumstances could the *querela inofficiosi testamenti* be brought at the time of Justinian? **(23)**
12. What was the *querela inofficiosae donationis*? **(23)**
13. Were there any restrictions on the type of property which could be given by way of *legatum per praeceptionem*? **(25)**
14. What was the effect of *Sc. Neronianum* on the law relating to legacies? **(26)**
15. State the general effect of *Lex Falcidia* on legacies. **(28)**
16. Outline the nature of codicils and trusts. **(30, 32)**
17. Explain (a) *bonorum possessio contra tabulas*, (b) *bonorum possessio secundum tabulas*. **(33)**

CHAPTER XIV

INTESTATE SUCCESSION

ITS NATURE

1. Meaning of intestacy. Intestate succession could occur where no will had been made, or, where having been made, the will lacked validity or failed eventually.

2. Partial intestacy. The general rule was that no one could die partly testate, partly intestate (*nemo pro parte testatus, pro parte intestatus decedere potest*). Hence, where a testator failed to make an effective disposition of his entire estate, the undisposed portion went, not to the heirs on intestacy, but to the testamentary heirs (*see* example at XII, **1**(c)).

3. The Law of intestate succession. This may be considered in three stages:

(a) *Under the XII Tables*—inheritance went to the family as constituted on the basis of *potestas*.

(b) *According to Praetorian Edict*—natural ties began to replace artificial ties.

(c) *Under Justinian*—relationship for purposes of inheritance was based on the blood tie, *potestas* being ignored.

UNDER THE XII TABLES

4. The general rule. "*Si intestato moritur cui suus heres nec escit, adgnatus proximus familiam habeto. Si adgnatus nec escit, gentiles familiam habento.*" ("If a man to whom there is no *suus heres* dies intestate, let the nearest agnate have the property. If there be no agnate, let the members of the *gens* have the property.") Hence, the order of succession was:

(a) *Sui heredes* (proper heirs).
(b) *Proximus adgnatus* (nearest agnate).
(c) *Gentiles* (members of the deceased man's *gens*).

5. Sui heredes. Under this classification came all those who, being free persons, but in the power of the deceased, would become *sui juris* by his death. Hence an adopted child of the intestate could succeed; but an emancipated son could not succeed, nor could a daughter of the deceased who was married and in *manus* of her husband (*see* VI, **14**).

NOTE: Posthumous children were *sui heredes* if they would have been so had they been born in the lifetime of the deceased.

There was no preference of male over female, and all *sui heredes* in the first degree of descent shared equally. Children in the second degree took as representatives of a dead parent *per stirpes* (by stems), so that the children together took their dead father's share.

6. Adgnati. After *sui heredes* the succession went to agnates (*see* V, **2**(b)), *i.e.* the nearest of those relatives who, if a common ancestor were alive, would be in his *potestas*. Preference was given to the nearest agnatic collateral (*proximus adgnatus*). Nearness in degree was computed according to the date of death, or according to the date on which the testamentary heir had refused to enter.

NOTE

(i) Agnates in the same degree shared not *per stirpes*, but *per capita* (by heads). There was no representation. Where the nearest agnatic collateral failed to enter, those in the next degree did not take.

(ii) Female agnates beyond the second degree could not succeed.

7. Gentiles (gens = a clan). Failing *adgnati*, men of the *gens* succeeded. The *gens* was a community to which deceased had belonged. This community consisted of a group of families with a common descent, a common name and probably a common worship and common tomb. In early times the *gens* was collectively responsible for the debts of its members and was obliged to ransom any members who had been made captives.

BY PRAETORIAN EDICT

8. Inadequacies of the Law of succession under the XII Tables. The decline of the *gens* and the inadequacies of agnatic succession made change inevitable. Agnatic succession involved injustice. Thus, female agnates beyond the degree of sister could not succeed; where the nearest agnate failed to enter, a remoter agnate could not succeed; an agnate who had suffered *capitis deminutio* (*see* IV, **6**) could not enter.

9. Bonorum Possessio (possession of goods). By Praetorian Edict *bonorum possessio intestati* was offered to four groups:

(a) *Unde liberi* (children) (*see* **11** below).
(b) *Unde legitimi* (nearest agnates and statutory heirs) (*see* **12** below).
(c) *Unde cognati* (blood relations in order of proximity) (*see* **13** below).
(d) *Unde vir et uxor* (husband and wife) (*see* **14** below).

> NOTE: *Unde* = by which. The word is included in the phrase "*Bonorum possessio ex illa parte edicti unde liberi (cognati, etc.) vocantur.*" ("Possession of goods under that part of the edict by which *liberi, cognati,* etc. are called.")

10. Limitation of time. Members of the four classes were allowed a time limit during which they had to apply for *bonorum possessio*. The period was fixed at 100 days; parents and children of the intestate were allowed one year. If no member of a class had applied within the fixed period members of the next class could apply. But those who had failed to apply in their correct class were allowed to claim in a later class.

11. Bonorum possessio unde liberi. In this class were *sui heredes* (*see* XIII, **4**), *emancipati* (emancipated children), children of deceased *emancipati*. Children given in adoption and remaining in another family were not included.

NOTE
  (i) Males and females were treated equally.
  (ii) Those in the same degree took *per stirpes* (by stems).
  (iii) An emancipated child who wished a grant of *bonorum possessio unde liberi* had to bring into hotchpot and make available for general distribution any property he had acquired after emancipation, with the exception of *peculium castrense* and *quasi-castrense* (*see* V, **4**). *See* also XIII, **33**(a).

12. Bonorum possessio unde legitimi. Those entitled under the XII Tables (*sui heredes, proximus adgnatus* and, at an early period, members of the deceased man's gens) could be granted *bonorum possessio unde legitimi*.

13. Bonorum possessio unde cognati. In this class were blood relations to the sixth degree and, in the case of children of second cousins, to the seventh degree. Hence, female agnates remoter than the sisters of the deceased were included. An adopted child was included. Remoter cognates were excluded by those in a nearer degree. Cognates of the same degree shared *per capita*.

14. Bonorum possessio unde vir et uxor. In the event of a failure of cognates husband and wife were given a reciprocal right of succession.

NOTE: The position of mother and child was as follows:
 (i) Under the civil law a mother who was not in the *manus* of her husband (*see* VI, **14**) had no claim. But by Praetorian Edict she could succeed in default of agnates as a cognate.
 (ii) By *Sc. Tertullianum* (*c.* A.D. 158) a mother who had *jus liberorum* (*i.e.* having had 3 children—4 in the case of a *libertina*—by separate births) had a right of succession after *sui heredes*, the father, and consanguineous brothers and sisters (who took together). The mother and sisters took half.
 (iii) By *Sc. Orphitianum* (A.D. 178) a child was given a first right of succession to its mother on her death intestate. The right was granted even where the child was not legitimate, provided that it was freeborn.

UNDER JUSTINIAN

15. The Novellae. By *Nov.* 118 (A.D. 543) and *Nov.* 127 A.D. 548) Justinian refashioned the order of succession. The result of this was:

(a) Agnation was replaced by a relationship based on the blood tie.
(b) Males and females were treated equally.
(c) A new order of succession appeared (*see* **16** below).

16. The order of succession. There were now four classes. Earlier classes excluded later ones and where members of an earlier class were unable or unwilling to accept, persons within the next class could claim.

(a) *The First Class: Descendants.* This class included those emancipated and not emancipated, adopted or natural, male and female. Those who succeeded in the first degree took *per capita*; those in a remoter degree took *per stirpes*. Nearer descendants excluded the more remote.

(b) *The Second Class: Ascendants and brothers and sisters of the whole blood.* Parents shared with brothers and sisters of the whole blood. A grandparent succeeded only where brothers, sisters and parents did not take. The child of a dead brother or sister represented its parents.

(c) *The Third Class: Brothers and sisters of the half blood.* Their children could take by representation.

(d) *The Fourth Class: All other collaterals.* Those in the same degree took *per capita*. There was no representation.

> NOTE: The next class to take would be husband and wife. They were not included in the *Novellae* of A.D. 543 and 548, but were mentioned in this connection in the *Basilica* (a restatement of the *Corpus Juris*, made at the order of the Emperor Basilius and published by his son Leo, c. A.D. 886).

OTHER TYPES OF SUCCESSION TO AN ENTIRE ESTATE

17. The estate of a freedman (*see* VIII, 12). Under the XII Tables a patron could succeed to his freedman's estate only where the freedman had died without making a will and without a *suus heres*. By Praetorian modification a freedman who had made a will had to leave half of his estate to his patron. The patron who had been left less than half was given *bonorum possessio contra tabulas* (*see* XIII, 33(a)). In the time of Gaius, where a freedman left an estate of less than 100 *aurei* and had made a will, the patron was excluded. Where the estate was more than 100 *aurei* and where there were children entitled to succeed, the patron and his issue were excluded.

18. The estate of a wife in manus marriage (*see* VI, 14). This estate passed to the husband or to the person who exercised *potestas* over the husband.

19. The estate of an adrogated person (*see* V, 8(a)). This passed to the *adrogator*.

20. The estate of a freewoman who cohabited with a slave (*see* VIII, 7(c)). After three denunciations by the slave's master, the woman's property was forfeited to the master, under *Sc. Claudianum* (A.D. 52). This was repealed by Justinian.

PROGRESS TEST 14

1. What was the order of succession on intestacy under the XII Tables? **(4)**

2. Explain the inadequacies of the law of succession on intestacy under the XII Tables. **(8)**

3. Explain (a) *bonorum possessio unde liberi,* (b) *bonorum possessio unde vir et uxor.* **(11, 14)**

4. What were the general results on intestate succession of *Novellae* 118 and 127? **(15)**

5. Outline the order of succession on intestacy under Justinian. **(16)**

6. What were the special rules attached to the disposition by will of a freedman's estate? **(17)**

PART FIVE

THE LAW OF OBLIGATIONS

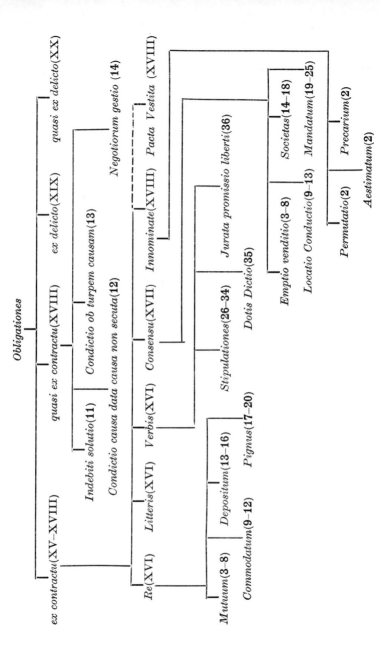

CHAPTER XV

THE NATURE OF OBLIGATIONS AND CONTRACTS

OBLIGATIONS

1. General. The Law of Property is concerned with rights *in rem*; the Law of Obligations is concerned with rights *in personam* (*see* XI, 1). The Law of Obligations is concerned specifically with the obligations arising out of contract and quasi-contract, considered in XVI–XVIII, and those arising out of delict and quasi-delict, considered in XIX–XX.

2. The concept of obligation. " *Obligatio est juris vinculum quo necessitate adstringimur alicuius solvendae rei, secundum nostrae civitatis jura.*"—The Institutes. ("An obligation is a legal bond whose force compels us to perform something in accordance with the laws of our state.") The essence of obligation is its personal nature. Obligations give rise to rights and duties.

> EXAMPLE: Brutus sells a horse to Publius. Brutus acquires a right to receive the agreed price from Publius and Publius acquires a right to take delivery of the horse. Brutus has the duty to give possession of the horse to Publius, and Publius has the duty to pay the agreed price.

3. Obligations classified.

(a) *Ex contractu; quasi ex contractu; ex delicto; quasi ex delicto·* (This is the classification used in the Institutes).
(b) *Civil obligations; natural obligations.* The first group comprises those protected by the law and giving rise to actions. In the second group are those which do not give rise to actions, but which may produce legally significant consequences, *e.g.* the case of a debt incurred by a child in *potestas.*
(c) *Obligationes civiles; obligationes honorariae.* The former

131

were based on *jus civile* (*see* II, **10**), the latter became actionable as a result of Edicts of the Praetors (*see* I, **13**).

THE NATURE OF CONTRACT

4. Definition. A contract came into existence in Roman Law when a person freely undertook a duty thereby intending to create a right *in personam* in favour of another person. The essence of a contractual agreement was, therefore, the creation of an obligation which would be enforced by the law.

> EXAMPLE: Cassius agrees with Brutus that he will sell to Brutus a slave, Menenius. As soon as the price is fixed the contract is complete. As a result Brutus acquires an actionable right *in personam* against Cassius for the delivery of Menenius. (When Menenius becomes his property he will acquire a right *in rem* in that property).

5. The basis of contract. Not every agreement was enforceable at law.

> EXAMPLE: Seius and Maevius agree to rob Flavius. Seius fails to carry out his part of the agreement. Maevius has no right of action against Seius (*see* (b) below).

In order that a contract might be valid, the following matters had to be observed:

(a) *The creation of legal relations* (*as opposed to, say, purely domestic agreements*) *had to be contemplated.* An agreement by Casca to accompany Trebonius to a performance of a drama would not be actionable if Casca failed to carry out his part of the agreement.

(b) *The object of the contract had to be legal and possible of achievement.*

(c) *Parties to the agreement had to enter freely, i.e.* neither fear nor force was to be used so as to induce agreement.

(d) *The agreement had to take a form recognised by law.*

(e) *There had to be consensus ad idem* (= agreement as to the same thing). Lack of *consensus* would vitiate the agreement and avoid the contract in the following cases:

> (i) Cassius buys a slave from Brutus. Cassius is under the impression that the slave in question is Stichus; Brutus assumes that the slave Cassius wishes to buy is Aulus.

This is a mistake *in corpore* (*i.e.* as to the subject matter of the contract).

(ii) Trebonius intends to let a house to Titius; Titius thinks he is buying the house. This is a mistake *in negotio* (*i.e.* as to the nature of the obligation).

(iii) Pindarus intends to lend a jewel to Clitus, but Lepidus fraudulently represents himself to Pindarus as Clitus and obtains the jewel. This illustrates a mistake *in persona* (*i.e.* as to the party to an agreement).

(iv) Marullus buys from Flavius a ring which he assumes is gold. The ring is lead. This is a mistake *in substantia* (*i.e.* as to the basic quality of the subject matter).

(f) *Parties to the contract had to have full contractual capacity.* The following persons, for example, lacked this capacity: Minors lacking a curator's consent (*see* VII, **13**); prodigals; lunatics; slaves; children under 7 (under Justinian) (*see* VII, **1**).

CLASSIFICATION OF CONTRACTS

6. In the Institutes. The classification adopted in the Institutes was:

(a) *Real:* arising from the delivery of a *res* (*see* XVI, **1–20**).

(b) *Literal:* arising from a particular type of writing (*see* XVI, **21–23**).

(c) *Verbal:* arising from a particular form of words (*see* XVI, **24–36**).

(d) *Consensual:* arising, in certain cases, from mere agreement (*see* XVII).

We shall add to these categories:

(e) *Innominate:* arising out of agreement and executed consideration (*see* XVIII, **1–3**).

(f) *Pacts:* arising out of agreements neither nominate nor innominate (*see* XVIII, **4–9**).

7. Formal or Informal. Where a contract arises out of its very form *e.g.* a stipulation (*see* XVI, **26**), it is said to be formal. Where a contract arises solely from the intentions of parties to the agreement (*e.g. emptio venditio*) (*see* XVII, **3**), it is said to be informal.

8. Unilateral or bilateral. A unilateral contract is an agreement in which the obligation of performance rests on one party, *e.g.* as in a contract for the loan of money, where the borrower has the obligation to repay. A bilateral contract, such as an agreement for the sale of a *res*, gave rise to reciprocal obligations: the buyer has the duty to pay the price, the vendor has the duty to deliver the *res*.

NOTE: A classification used to describe actions as *bonae fidei* or *stricti juris* was also used to describe some contracts. Contracts *stricti juris* bound the person who made a promise to perform exactly that which he had promised. In an action arising on such a contract an *exceptio* could be pleaded by way of defence (*see* XXII, **23**). In the case of contracts *bonae fidei*, the *judex* would take into account equitable defences, even where these were not pleaded specifically. Thus, unilateral contracts were usually enforced by actions *stricti juris*, bilateral contracts by actions *bonae fidei*.

THE EXTINCTION OF OBLIGATIONS

9. General. Obligations could be determined in several ways, *e.g.*

(a) By death and *capitis deminutio* (*see* **10** below).
(b) By actual performance or equivalents (*see* **11** below).
(c) By formal and non-formal releases (*see* **12** below).
(d) By *confusio* (*see* **13** below).
(e) By *litis contestatio* (*see* **14** below).
(f) By prescription (*see* **15** below).
(g) By novation (*see* **16** below).

10. Death and capitis deminutio. Where the obligations of either party were of a purely personal nature and could not be transmitted to an heir, they were extinguished on the death of either party. *Capitis deminutio* as a result of adrogation extinguished certain debts (*see* V, **8**(a) (iii)).

11. Actual performance or equivalents.

(a) *Performance (solutio). Solutio* was the performance of the obligation. Where a promise was of a personal service, only the promisor's personal performance extinguished the obligation. Payment, in performance of an obligation, could be made by a third party even without the knowledge, or against the will of the debtor. The time at which the debt was to fall due was determined by the terms of the obligation; the place of performance was determined in the same way.

(b) *Tender* (*oblatio*). *Oblatio* was a simple offer to pay. Formal tender was effected by depositing the money in a sealed bag in a temple or elsewhere, according to judicial order. Such a deposit released the debtor.

(c) *Impossibility of performance*. When the impossibility arose subsequent to the agreement, the promisor was discharged, as when, for example, A agrees to deliver goods to B and, through no fault of A, the goods perish before the delivery can be made.

12. Formal and non-formal release.

(a) *Acceptilatio* (*formal release of a stipulation*). This was a fictitious payment effected by a formal question and answer. Suppose that Brutus has entered into a stipulation (*see* XVI, **26**) under which he is to pay Aulus 100 *aurei*, and that Aulus has later agreed to release Brutus from his debt. Under this mode of release Brutus would say, "That which I have promised to you, do you regard as received?" Aulus would reply, "I do." An indivisible obligation could not be released in this mode except by an *acceptilatio* covering the entire obligation.

(b) *Nexi liberatio*, or *solutio per aes et libram* (*release by bronze and balance*). Before Justinian there existed, as a mode of release from debt, a ceremony of fictitious repayment involving the use of bronze and balance before five witnesses and a *libripens*, as in *mancipatio* (*see* X, **12**). The debtor was discharged after the recital of an appropriate formula. This mode of release was used in the case of a debt contracted *per aes et libram*, or in the case of a judgment debt.

(c) *Non-formal release*. Under the early law obligations arising *ex delicto* (*see* XX) could be released by informal agreement. Justinian allowed consensual contracts (*see* XVII) to be ended by an informal release where the obligations under the contract were outstanding on both sides.

13. Confusio (merger). Where, for example, a creditor became the heir of his debtor, or a debtor became the heir of his creditor, the debt, as such, was extinguished.

14. Litis contestatio (joinder of issue) (*see* XXII, **16**). In an action to enforce a contract the original claim was considered as extinguished after the plaintiff had been given his formula and a *judex* had been nominated (*see* also **16**(c) below).

15. Prescription. In A.D. 424 Theodosius fixed a period of 30 years for the extinction of actions *in personam*. Justinian fixed a period of 30 years for all actions (except the *actio hypothecaria*—40 years). Prescription was to run from the time at which the right of action came into existence; in the case of a conditional obligation it ran from the time when the condition was fulfilled. An acknowledgment by the debtor of the debt interrupted the period of prescription and created a new point in time at which a new prescriptive period started. The prescriptive period which applied to actions brought by the *Fiscus* (Treasury) was 20 years, with the exception of taxes, which were imprescriptible.

16. Novation.

(a) Novation involves the dissolving of an old obligation by the creation of a new one.

> EXAMPLE: Aulus owes Brutus 200 *aurei*. Brutus can transfer his right to receive the debt to Claudius and, in that case, Aulus becomes the debtor of Claudius. Alternatively, Brutus may agree to accept Dardanius as his debtor in place of Aulus.

(b) The consent of all parties was needed for the substitution of a creditor, but it was possible to substitute a new debtor without the old debtor's consent.

(c) *Novatio necessaria* (as contrasted with *novatio voluntaria* in (a) above) was the result of *litis contestatio* (*see* **14** above). The existing obligation was extinguished and replaced by an obligation to accept the result of the action.

THE INSOLVENT DEBTOR

17. Under the XII Tables. After the acknowledgment of his debt, and after judgment was given against him, the debtor had 30 days in which to pay. Following this period he was arrested, brought before a magistrate and placed in chains

THE LAW OF OBLIGATIONS

(*manus injectio*) (*see* also **XXI, 10**). After a further two months he could be sold into slavery or be put to death.

18. Lex Poetelia (c. 326 B.C.). The property of a debtor, but not his body, was liable in the case of failure to repay a loan of money.

19. Bonorum emptio (purchase of property). The Praetor granted *missio in possessionem*, by which creditors entered into possession of the debtor's estate for thirty days, during which public notice of the seizure of the estate was given. A public auction followed, after which the debtor incurred *infamia* (*see* **VI, 11**(e)). After another interval the estate was sold in one lot to the highest bidder and the creditors received their dividend.

20. Bonorum cessio (cession of goods). Under Augustus an insolvent debtor whose insolvency was not the result of his *culpa* (negligence) could avoid *infamia* by voluntarily surrendering his property to his creditors.

21. Bonorum distractio (distraint on goods). In the later Roman Law the property of an insolvent debtor was entrusted to a *curator bonorum* appointed by the creditors. The *curator* was obliged to sell the property in separate lots and to pay the creditors *pro rata*. The debtor avoided *infamia*.

22. Complete discharge. This was possible only after all debts had been paid. Actions to recover outstanding debts would be brought against a debtor who had acquired property after the proceedings described in **19–21** above.

PROGRESS TEST 15

1. "The Law of Property is concerned with rights *in rem*; the Law of Obligations with rights *in personam*." Explain. **(1)**
2. "Obligations give rise to rights and duties." Explain. **(2)**
3. What was the essence of a contractual agreement in Roman Law? **(4)**
4. Ligarius and Lepidus make a solemn agreement to rob Caius and to share the proceeds of the robbery. Can such an agreement be considered as a contract? **(5)**

5. What was meant by full contractual capacity? In whom was it lacking? (5)

6. What was meant by *consensus ad idem*? Is *consensus ad idem* present where Pindarus intends to buy a field from Dardanius and Dardanius is under the impression that he is letting the field to Pindarus? (5)

7. Explain the difference between unilateral and bilateral contracts. (8)

8. Enumerate the ways in which obligations could be extinguished. (9)

9. Explain the effect on debts of *capitis deminutio*. (10)

10. Outline the effect of prescription on obligations. (15)

11. Explain *bonorum emptio*. (19)

12. Under what circumstances might *distractio bonorum* take place? (21)

CHAPTER XVI

CONTRACTS—1: REAL, LITERAL AND VERBAL CONTRACTS

OBLIGATIONES RE

1. General. "Real" contracts (the word "real" is derived from *res*) have a common basis: they involve agreement and the transfer from one person to another of a *res corporalis* (*see* IX, 3). Although agreement is essential to the formation of a real contract, the actual obligation depends on the transfer of a *res*. The essence of the obligation is the return of the *res*, or its equivalent.

2. The four real contracts.

(a) *Mutuum* (*see* **3–8** below).
(b) *Commodatum* (*see* **9–12** below).
(c) *Depositum* (*see* **13–16** below).
(d) *Pignus* (*see* **17–20** below).

MUTUUM

3. Its meaning. *Mutuum* (a loan) is a gratuitous loan for consumption of *res quae usu consumuntur* (*see* IX, **12**). It involves the transfer of the ownership of money, or other fungible things, from X to Y with the intention that Y should return to X the precise sum of money or, in the case of *res* other than money, things of the same quantity, quality and kind. *Mutuum* was a unilateral contract (*see* XV, **8**), the sole obligation rested on Y to return the *res*, or its equivalent, to X.

4. Duties of the borrower.

(a) He was bound to restore to the lender the same type of thing which he had borrowed. In the case of money the same amount (not the same coins) had to be restored.

139

(b) He could be required to pay interest (*see* **6** below) if there had been a special stipulation (*see* **26** below) to that effect.

5. Restrictions. Persons in *potestas* (*see* V) were not allowed to accept a loan of money. *Sc. Macedonianum* (*c.* A.D. 69) prohibited actions for the recovery of money from sons in *potestas*. The loan was not void, but the lender was denied an action.

There were exceptions to the rule in the following cases:

(a) Where the loan had been made with the consent of a *paterfamilias*, or where he had ratified it.
(b) Where the son had borrowed to pay a legal debt.
(c) Where the loan was for the benefit of the *paterfamilias*.
(d) Where the creditor had made a reasonable mistake, or had been misled, as to the borrower's status.
(e) Where the son had borrowed on his *peculium* (*see* V, **4**).
(f) Where the loan was to a son who, being abroad, had borrowed to pay for his education or official duties.
(g) Where the son acknowledged the debt by part payment or ratification after he became *sui juris*.

6. Rates of interest. Interest (*fenus*) had to be the subject of a special stipulation. Under the XII Tables it was limited to 12%. In 345 B.C. this was reduced to 6%. *Lex Genucia* (340 B.C.) prohibited it. Under Justinian, interest was not allowed to be recovered to a greater amount than twice the principal; compound interest was forbidden. The rates in Justinian's time were:

Maritime loans:	12% *p.a.*
Business loans:	8% *p.a.*
Ordinary, non-business loans:	6% *p.a.*
Loans to farmers and persons of high rank:	4% *p.a.*

7. Maritime loans. *Pecunia trajectitia* (*trajectio* = a crossing by sea) was a loan of money to finance the purchase and shipping of merchandise at the lender's risk. The loan was not repaid unless the goods arrived at their destination in safety.

8. Actions. The lender had an *actio certae pecuniae creditae*, in the case of money, or *condictio triticaria*, in the case of other *res*. In the former action the lender could challenge the borrower to a wager of one-third of the loan; if the lender suc-

ceeded he received the loan plus the wager, but if he failed he
was liable to the borrower for the amount of the wager.

COMMODATUM

9. Its meaning. *Commodatum* was the gratuitous loan of a
res for use. It gave rise to obligations and rights for both
parties. The lender was the *commodans*, the borrower was the
commodatarius.

10. Duties of the lender.

(a) To allow the borrower to enjoy the use of the *res*.
(b) To pay any extraordinary expenses involved in preserving
the *res*.
(c) To pay for any damage resulting from defects in the *res*.

11. Duties of the borrower.

(a) To return the *res*, *in specie* and not *in genere*, and in as good
condition as when received, except for ordinary wear and
tear.
(b) To use the *res* only as agreed upon.
(c) To exercise *exacta diligentia* (*i.e.* the standard of care
shown by a *bonus paterfamilias* in the conduct of his
affairs). He was liable for *culpa* (*i.e.* for those faults which
a *bonus paterfamilias* would not commit) but was not
liable for the destruction of the *res* as the result of events
beyond his control.

12. Actions. The duties of the borrower were enforced by the
actio commodati directa; the duties of the lender were enforced
by the *actio commodati contraria* and the *actio utilis commodati
contraria*. In the case of a lender who had seized the *res* lent,
without the borrower's knowledge, and had sued the borrower
for its value, the *actio utilis* enforced a restoration of the price
to the borrower.

DEPOSITUM

13. Its meaning. *Depositum* was a contract in which a depositor gave a *res* to a depositee to be kept without remunera-

tion and to be returned on demand. Special cases of *depositum* were:

(a) *Depositum sequestre.* Where the ownership of a *res* was the subject of litigation, the *res* could be deposited with a third party until the action was settled. The *sequester* was often appointed by a *judex*. The contract could be enforced by an *actio sequestraria.*

(b) *Depositum necessarium.* In the case of fire, shipwreck or civil disturbance, goods might be deposited. Double damages could be claimed if the property deposited was not returned on demand.

(c) *Depositum irregulare.* In this case the *res* had to be returned *in genere* (in kind), *e.g.* money deposited in a bank.

14. Duties of the depositor.

(a) To pay any expenses involved in the custody of the *res*.
(b) To make good any damage caused by the *res*.

15. Duties of the depositee.

(a) To keep the *res* safely and not to use it.
(b) To return the *res* and its produce on demand without charge. An unreasonable refusal made him liable to pay interest.
(c) To give the depositor any of his rights of action against a person who had caused the loss of the *res*.

16. Actions. The duties of the depositee were enforced by an *actio depositi directa*, in which condemnation brought *infamia* (*see* VI, **11**(e)). The duties of the depositor were enforced by an *actio depositi contraria.*

PIGNUS

17. Its meaning. The transfer of a *res corporalis* to a creditor as security for a debt, with a condition of its return on payment of the debt (*see* also XI, **14**).

18. Duties of the debtor.

(a) To indemnify the creditor for any damage caused by the *res*.
(b) To pay any expenses involved.

19. Duties of the creditor.

(a) To return the *res* when the debt was paid.

(b) To exercise *exacta diligentia* (*see* **11**(c) above). He had to realise any fruits of the property and set this off against interest and capital. The *pactum antichreseos* allowed him to retain fruits in lieu of the interest.

(c) To use the *res* only if authorised by the agreement. To do otherwise was construed as theft.

20. Actions. The duties of the creditor were enforced by the *actio pigneraticia directa*; the duties of the debtor were enforced by the *actio pigneraticia contraria*.

OBLIGATIONES LITTERIS

21. General. The domestic account books of a *paterfamilias* in the early Republic included the *adversaria*, or daybook, in which daily transactions were recorded, and the *codex accepti et expensi*, in which monthly payments and receipts were recorded. Entries in the *codex* were known as *nomina arcaria* and were statements of claims, which were evidence of obligations.

22. Expensilatio. This was the creation of a literal contract by a debit entry made with the debtor's consent by the creditor in his *codex*. The *nomen transscriptitium* thus created gave rise to legal liability.

NOTE

(i) This was the only written contract in Roman Law.

(ii) *Nomen transscriptitium* applied to Roman citizens only. For peregrines, literal contracts in the form of *syngraphae* and *chirographa* (written acknowledgment of debts) were available.

(iii) The appropriate action was the *actio certae creditae pecuniae*.

(iv) The literal contract had disappeared by the end of the classical period.

23. Under Justinian. In the time of Justinian *cautiones* (written acknowledgments of debts) were in regular use. A debtor who was sued on the evidence of a *cautio* could plead an *exceptio doli* (defence alleging fraud by the plaintiff) or the *querela non numeratae pecuniae* (complaint that money had not been paid). The *querela* had to be pleaded within two years of the date of the *cautio*. An unsuccessful defendant who had denied the written instrument, or, having admitted it, claimed that he had not received the sum in question, was liable in twofold damages.

OBLIGATIONES VERBIS

24. General. A verbal contract arises out of a declaration of words, the declaration being in a set form. The obligation is created by the form.

25. The verbal contracts.

(a) *Stipulatio* (*see* **26–34** below).
(b) *Dotis dictio* (*see* **35** below).
(c) *Jurata promissio liberti* (*see* **36** below).

STIPULATIONES CONVENTIONALES

26. General. Stipulations were formal, unilateral contracts. *Stipulationes conventionales* (as opposed to those considered in **29–31** below) resulted from voluntary agreement of the parties. They could be used for any type of agreement and imposed on the promisor the duty to give or to do that which he had promised.

27. Form of the stipulation. A solemn question and answer formed the stipulation. The stipulator asked the question; the promisor was the person bound by the answer. Hence, "to stipulate" in this sense meant to ask for a promise. A creditor, for example, would be the stipulator; the debtor would be the promisor. Certain words had to be incorporated in the question and answer, *e.g.*:

(a) *Spondesne?* (Do you pledge your word?) *Spondeo* (I pledge my word).

> NOTE: This form, religious in origin, was available to Roman citizens only. Aliens could use the forms below, or their equivalents in Greek.

(b) *Promittis?* (Do you promise?) *Promitto* (I promise).
(c) *Facies?* (Will you do?) *Faciam* (I will do).

NOTE
 (i) Question and answer had to be consecutive, with no intervening action.
 (ii) Parties had to be within hearing distance of each other. Deaf and dumb persons could not use this form.
 (iii) Question and answer had to agree. At a later stage in the law, however, where A stated, "Do you promise 100 *aurei*?" and B replied, "I promise 80 *aurei*," the stipulation for 80 *aurei* was valid.
 (iv) In A.D. 472 Leo II enacted that the strict forms need not be used. A stipulation would be binding if question and answer had been used and the intention of the parties was clear.
 (v) No witnesses were required to a stipulation.

28. Actions. *Condictio triticaria* was available for the enforcement of a promise to give a specific *res*. *Certae Pecuniae* was available for the enforcement of a promise to pay money. The *actio ex stipulatu* was available to enforce a promise to do, or refrain from doing, a particular act.

STIPULATIONES JUDICIALES, PRAETORIAE, COMMUNES

29. Stipulationes judiciales. These stipulations were entered into by the order of a *judex*, *e.g.*

(a) *De persequendo servo restituendove pretio.* A stipulation to pursue a runaway slave, or to return his price.
(b) *De dolo cautio.* A security against fraud.

30. Stipulationes praetoriae. The Praetor might call for stipulations, *e.g.*

(a) *Stipulatio damni infecti.* Security for compensation in the event of damage to one's house or land, *e.g.* as the result of constructions upon neighbouring land.
(b) *Stipulatio legatorum servandorum causa.* Security for legacies in the case of an heir bound to pay a legacy and obliged to enter into a stipulation to do so.

F

31. Stipulationes communes. Either the Praetor or a *judex* might demand certain stipulations, *e.g.*

(a) *Stipulatio de rato.* Security given by a *procurator* (*see* X, 22) that his acts would be ratified by his principal.
(b) *Stipulatio pupilli rem salvam fore.* A stipulation for the security of a pupil's property, entered into by his *tutor* (*see* VII, 8).

INVALID STIPULATIONS

32. Grounds of invalidity.
(a) The subject matter, *e.g.* its non-existence.
(b) The persons between whom the stipulation was made, *e.g.* master and slave.
(c) The manner in which it was made, *e.g.* parties not *ad idem* (*see* XV, 5(e)).
(d) A condition subject to which the stipulation was made, *e.g.* an illegal condition.

ADSTIPULATIO

33. Its meaning. Where two or more persons joined in making a stipulation, they were known as adstipulators, and the stipulation was known as an *adstipulatio* (adstipulation). Each of the adstipulators could enforce the stipulation against the promisor. The promisor was discharged by performance of the promise on the demand of one of the adstipulators. Adstipulation was used to enforce a stipulation in the absence of a principal stipulator, or in the event of his death. The fraudulent release of a debtor by an adstipulator rendered him liable to penalties in an action by the principal stipulator (*see* XIX, 8(b) (ii)).

STIPULATIONS OF SLAVES

34. General rules.

(a) A slave was able to stipulate for his master, using his master's name or his own, even though the master knew nothing of it. In such a case the master obtained the benefit of the stipulation (*see* XVII, 25(c)).
(b) A stipulation by the slave for a stranger was void.

(c) A slave who belonged to an inheritance could stipulate for the benefit of that inheritance.

(d) Where a slave was owned in common by more than one master, the masters acquired the benefits of the stipulation in proportion to their interests in him, unless he had stipulated on behalf of one master (who would then acquire the benefit).

OTHER VERBAL CONTRACTS

35. Dotis Dictio (*see* VI, 26). This was a formal, spoken covenant entered into by an intended wife, or her father, or other male ascendant, to confer a dowry. Following an enactment of Theodosius II (A.D. 428), informal agreement was sufficient.

36. Jurata promissio liberti. When a slave was manumitted (*see* VIII, **9, 12**), he was obliged to promise services (*obligatio operarum*) to his former master. This verbal promise on oath was repeated after manumission.

PROGRESS TEST 16

1. What was a "real" contract? Enumerate the four real contracts. (**1, 2**)

2. Define *Mutuum*. What were the borrower's duties? (**3, 4**)

3. Outline the provisions of *Sc. Macedonianum*. (**5**)

4. Define *Commodatum*. What were the borrower's duties? (**9, 11**)

5. Explain (a) *actio certae pecuniae creditae,* (b) *actio commodati directa.* (**8, 12**)

6. What was meant by (a) *depositum necessarium,* (b) *depositum irregulare*? (**13**)

7. What were the duties of the depositor? How could these duties be enforced? (**14, 16**)

8. Explain (a) *nomina arcaria,* (b) *nomen transscriptitium.* (**21, 22**)

9. What was a verbal contract? (**24**)

10. "A stipulation was a formal unilateral contract." Comment. (**26**)

11. What was the effect of the following stipulation: Brutus:

"Do you promise 200 *aurei*?" Cassius: "I promise 150 *aurei*"? **(27)**

12. Give examples of (a) *stipulationes praetoriae*, (b) *stipulatio de rato*. **(30, 31)**

13. On what grounds might a stipulation be invalid? **(32)**

14. What was the meaning of adstipulation? **(33)**

15. Could a slave enter into a stipulation? **(34)**

CHAPTER XVII

CONTRACTS—2: CONSENSUAL CONTRACTS

OBLIGATIONES CONSENSU

1. General. The basis of the consensual contracts was mere agreement (*nudo consensu*). No physical act, *e.g.* of transfer, was necessary to give rise to the contract, and form was not important.

2. The four consensual contracts.

(a) *Emptio venditio* (*see* **3–8** below).
(b) *Locatio conductio* (*see* **9–13** below).
(c) *Societas* (*see* **14–18** below).
(d) *Mandatum* (*see* **19–25** below).

EMPTIO VENDITIO

3. Its meaning. *Emptio venditio* (sale) was a contract in which the seller (*venditor*) agreed to give exclusive possession of a *res* to the buyer (*emptor*) for a price (*pretium*). No formalities were required, but, under Justinian, if parties had agreed to reduce the agreement into writing, it was not held to be binding until they had signed, and either party could withdraw before the agreement had been put into writing. Where there was no writing the contract was held to be complete on determination of the subject matter and its price.

4. Essentials of the contract.

(a) *Res.* The thing to be sold had to be in existence and capable of being the subject of ownership. It had to be specific, *e.g.* "that brooch," or "100 bushels of wheat in your granary," and not merely generic, *e.g.* "a brooch," or "100 bushels of wheat." In some cases the sale of "future commodities" was possible: X might contract to sell Y the next year's crop from X's orchards. In such a case, where it was intended that the seller should bear the risk of the total failure of the crop, the sale was known as *emptio rei speratae* (sale of an expected thing) and the agreement was void if there was no crop. Where it was intended that the buyer should bear the risk, the sale was known as *emptio spei* (sale of an expectation) and the buyer had to pay even if the crop failed completely.

(b) *Price.* The price had to be definite, genuine, and in coined money. In the case of land the price had to be reasonable (*justum*). Where the vendor of land complained of *laesio enormis* (more than ordinary prejudice), in that the agreed price was less than half the real value of the *res*, he could claim the right to rescind, unless the purchaser was prepared to pay an increased price.

(c) *Agreement.* Unconditional and definite agreement as to the *res* to be sold and the price was required.

> NOTE: *Arra confirmatoria* consisted of coins given as "earnest" to confirm the contract. *Arra poenitentialis*, introduced at a later date, was considered as an instalment of the price. If the seller failed to complete, the buyer could claim double the *arra*; if the buyer failed to complete, the *arra* passed to the seller.

5. Duties of the buyer.

(a) To pay the agreed price.
(b) To accept delivery at the agreed time.
(c) To pay expenses involved in keeping the *res* after contract and prior to delivery.

6. Duties of the seller.

(a) To deliver the *res* at the agreed time.
(b) To exercise *exacta diligentia* (*see* XVI, **11**(c)) pending delivery.
(c) To give exclusive and vacant possession, *i.e.* to guarantee against eviction by order of the court. Damages on eviction equalled the market value of the property at the time of eviction.
(d) To suffer rescission or offer compensation where the *res* had undisclosed defects which interfered with its enjoyment. Originally the vendor was bound by undertakings at the

time of sale, but not for any latent defects in the *res* sold.
The purchaser, however, could guard himself by stipulations. At a later stage the *Curule Aediles* (*see* I, **11(f)**) introduced a requirement that vendors of slaves and animals
should disclose publicly certain defects, *e.g.* disease. The
actio redhibitoria, for rescission, could be brought within
6 months where defects were revealed. An alternative
action could be brought within one year for a reduction in
price. In time these remedies covered all types of goods
sold.

7. Conditions in contracts of sale. A sale might be subject to
suspensive conditions (in which case no obligation arose until
the conditions were satisfied), or resolutive conditions (in
which case the sale could be rescinded on the happening of
particular events). Examples of this are:

(a) *Pactum displicentiae.* A resolutive condition under which
   a buyer might rescind by returning the goods to the seller,
   if he found them unsatisfactory.

(b) *Lex commissoria.* A resolutive condition, under which
   the purchase money had to be paid by a stated date, in
   default of which the sale could be declared void by the
   seller.

(c) *Addictio in diem.* A suspensive or resolutive condition by
   which parties agreed that the sale should be good, or remain good, save where the vendor sells the *res* at a higher
   price to another purchaser by a stated date.

(d) *Emptio ad gustum.* A suspensive or resolutive condition by
   which the vendor must sell if the buyer expresses satisfaction with the *res*, or by which the buyer can avoid the
   contract by declaring his rejection of the thing sold by, for
   example, sampling grain.

8. Actions.

(a) *Actio empti*, by which the seller was compelled to perform
   his part of the agreement or pay compensation.

(b) *Actio redhibitoria*, by which the buyer could rescind within
   6 months of the sale (*see* **6(d)** above).

(c) *Actio aestimatoria seu quanti minoris*, brought for a reduction in price because of defects, within one year.

(d) *Actio venditi,* by which the buyer was compelled to perform his part of the agreement.

> NOTE: *Periculum rei* (risk of the property) passed to the buyer as soon as the contract was complete. But in four cases the risk remained with the seller:
> (i) in the case of a *res* sold under a condition (*see* 7 above), until that condition had been fulfilled;
> (ii) in the case of things sold by weight or measure, until they had been ascertained;
> (iii) in the case of a *venditor in mora* (*i.e.* a seller who had wilfully delayed carrying out his duties);
> (iv) in the case of an agreement giving the buyer a choice of two *res*—but here the loss fell on the buyer if both *res* perished.

LOCATIO CONDUCTIO

9. Its meaning. *Locatio conductio* (hire) was a contract whereby one party (*locator*) agreed to give to another (*conductor*) the use of something, or to perform some service in return for a fixed sum (*merces certa*). There were three types of *locatio conductio*:

(a) *Locatio conductio rei,* in which the *locator* lets to the *conductor* the use of a *res corporalis* or *incorporalis.*
(b) *Locatio conductio operarum,* in which the *locator* puts his services, or those of his slave, at the disposal of the *conductor.* (In this case the employee is the *locator.*)
(c) *Locatio conductio operis,* in which the *locator* puts out work to be performed by the *conductor.* (In this case the employer is the *locator.*)

The contract of hire required no formalities and was complete when agreement had been reached.

10. Duties of the locator.

(a) *In the case of locatio conductio of things:*
  (i) To deliver the *res* to the hirer and to allow him to keep it for the agreed time.
  (ii) To look after the *res* so that it can be used.
  (iii) To compensate for injuries resulting from defects in the *res.*
  (iv) To guarantee against eviction arising from his defaults.

(b) *In the case of locatio conductio of services:*

   (i) To execute the work properly and within a reasonable time.

  (ii) To take good care of those things entrusted to him.

> NOTE: The *locator* in this case was not liable for loss of a *res* resulting from robbery; nor was he liable for loss resulting from faults in the materials on which he was working.

> EXAMPLE: Brutus sends a precious stone to Publius to be set in a brooch. Publius breaks the stone. He must pay damages to Brutus if the breaking was the result of his carelessness, but not if it resulted from a flaw in the stone.

11. Duties of the conductor.

(a) *In the case of locatio conductio of things:*

   (i) To take reasonable care of the *res*. He was responsible if the *res* was stolen, but not if it was seized by robbers.

  (ii) To keep possession of the *res* for the time agreed upon.

 (iii) To pay the agreed rent, plus interest, where payment was in arrears. The rent had to be certain, genuine, and in money (but *see* note below). *Laesio enormis* did not apply. He could be evicted after two years for non-payment of rent.

 (iv) To surrender the *res* at the end of the agreed period.

  (v) To carry out small repairs.

> NOTE: In the case of a tenancy of agricultural land, the rent could be paid in the form of produce, either as a fixed proportion (*pars quota*) of the annual harvest, or as an absolute portion (*pars quanta*) from specified land, *e.g.* "a quarter of the grain produced in each harvest," or, "100 bushels of grain each year."

(b) *In the case of locatio conductio of services:*

   (i) To pay the wages agreed.

  (ii) To pay interest if the wages were not paid at the correct time.

12. Determination of locatio conductio.

(a) *By confusio (merger), e.g.* by one and the same person becoming conductor and locator.

(b) *By destruction of the res.*

(c) *By expiration of an agreed time.*

(d) *By consent of both parties.*

(e) *By death of a workman;* but not by death of a letter or hirer of a thing. Where a hirer died, his heir took over his rights and duties.

(f) *By just cause, e.g.* eviction after non-payment of rent for two years, or if the premises were not being kept in proper repair.

13. Actions. *Actio locati* was available to the *locator. Actio conducti* was available to the *conductor.*

NOTE

(i) Remission of rent could be claimed in the case of failure of crops resulting from *vis major*, such as floods or earthquakes.

(ii) In the case of professional services given by a member of the upper classes on behalf of another person, *e.g.* as an advocate, the custom was to give such services gratuitously. By custom also he received a presentation (*honorarium*) from the person who had received the services.

(iii) The jettison of cargo from a hired ship was governed by *Lex Rhodia de jactu* (based on the maritime laws of Rhodes). Where some of a ship's cargo was jettisoned so as to save the ship, the owners of the jettisoned goods could claim compensation from the owner of the ship and from the owner of the cargo. The value of the jettisoned goods was the price paid for them; the value of the goods saved was the price they fetched at their destination.

(iv) In the case of a workman who made articles with his own materials, the question arose: was this a sale of materials or a hire of his labour? It was decided that it was a contract of sale. If the workman supplied only his labour it was a contract of hire.

SOCIETAS

14. Its meaning. *Societas* (partnership) was a contract by which two or more persons, with a common purpose in view, combined their property, or by which one contributed his labour and another his property. The contract was bilateral (*see* XV, **8**) and was completed by agreement without formalities. The partnership depended on the continuing consent of the partners; the partnership could be dissolved by one partner declaring his intention to retire (*see* **17** below). *Affectio societas* (intention to create a partnership) was essential. Each partner had to make a contribution to the venture and the object of the partnership had to be legal.

15. Types of Societas.

(a) *Societas universorum quae ex quaestu veniunt* (*professional or trade partnership*). This was the type of partnership which arose in business transactions, *e.g.* among bankers. Each partner contributed property and profits were divided in proportion to shares.

(b) *Societas negotiationis alicujus* (*partnership for a single transaction*). Such a partnership could be limited to one transaction, *e.g.* a sale.

(c) *Societas vectigalis* (*partnership for collection of taxes*). The state's taxes were farmed out to *publicani,* who formed themselves into companies for the purpose.

(d) *Societas universorum bonorum* (*universal partnership*). This partnership concerned all the property of the partners. Immediately the contract was made all the partners' property became their joint property. All lawful expenses of the partners were met from the common fund. Rights of action by each partner were at the disposal of all the partners.

(e) *Societas unius rei vel certarum rerum* (*joint ownership in relation to a single thing*). This involved joint ownership of a *res* arising from an agreement between the parties. It was not really a partnership, but was considered as such because the parties could employ an *actio pro socio* for an account among themselves.

NOTE: The so-called *societas leonina*, in which a partner was excluded from any share in the profits, was held to be void.

16. Duties of Partners.

(a) To contribute their agreed shares to the common partnership fund.

(b) To contribute to the common fund anything obtained in respect of the partnership.

(c) To share as agreed in profits and losses of the partnership.

(d) To indemnify one another against expenses incurred for the partnership.

(e) To exercise in the affairs of the partnership *diligentia quam suis rebus* (*i.e.* the care one should habitually show in managing one's own affairs) and to be liable for *dolus* (wilful default).

> NOTE: Partners were not considered as agents of the partnership, hence one partner could not bind his co-partners.

17. Termination of societas.

(a) *Ex actione.* For a *socius* (partner) to bring an action for his rights was tantamount to declaring an intention to dissolve the partnership.
(b) *Ex rebus.* The partnership terminated when the object for which it had been formed was achieved, or had become impossible to achieve, or as a result of the loss of the partnership's property.
(c) *Ex voluntate.* Express renunciation, or the expiration of an agreed period of time, ended the partnership.
(d) *Ex personis.* The death of a partner dissolved the partnership (except in the case of *societas vectigalis*). *Capitis deminutio* (*see* IV, **6**), bankruptcy, confiscation of goods, produced the same effect.

18. Actions. The *actio pro socio* was available to enforce a partner's rights. Condemnation brought *infamia* (*see* VI, **11**(e)). The *actio communi dividundo* was available for division of the partnership property.

MANDATUM

19. Its meaning. *Mandatum* (mandate) was a contract in which one party (*mandatarius*) promised to give or do something, without any remuneration, at the request of the other party (*mandator*). Such a contract required no formalities, consent being sufficient to establish the mandate. Agreement might be implied from the conduct of the parties. The object of a mandate had to be lawful and it was also essential that the *mandator* should have some interest in that which was to be done by the *mandatarius*.

20. Types of mandate.

(a) In the interests of the *mandator*.
(b) In the interests of the *mandator* and *mandatarius*.

(c) In the interests of the *mandator* and a third party.

(d) In the interests of a third party.

(e) In the interests of the *mandatarius* and a third party.

> NOTE: a mandate in the interests of the *mandatarius* alone was not binding.

21. Duties of the mandatarius.

(a) To carry out that which he had undertaken to do, with reservation of a right of renunciation, which could be exercised only where it did not prejudice the *mandator*.

(b) To keep to, and not exceed, the terms of the mandate.

(c) To surrender to the *mandator* anything acquired in the performance of the mandate.

(d) To render an account when called upon to do so.

(e) To take care of property received and to exercise *exacta diligentia* (see XVI, 11(c)).

22. Duties of the mandator.

(a) To compensate the *mandatarius* for expenses involved in carrying out the mandate.

(b) To indemnify the *mandatarius* for any liabilities incurred.

23. Termination of mandatum.

(a) By revocation or renunciation.

(b) By performance.

(c) By lapse of agreed period of time.

(d) By death of *mandator* or *mandatarius* (but not if the mandate continued to be carried out in ignorance of the death of the *mandator*).

24. Actions. The *actio mandata directa* was available for the *mandator*. A wilful breach of duty by the *mandatarius* resulted in *infamia* (see VI, 11(e)).

25. The main objects for which mandatum might be employed.

(a) *To transfer the benefit of an obligation, e.g.* a debt. In such a case, the assignee received a mandate to sue in the name of the assignor.

(b) *To create suretyship, i.e.* a contract by which a surety bound himself to answer for a principal's debt.

NOTE

    (i) Under Hadrian a surety had the right of *beneficium divisionis* by which the claims of a creditor were shared equally among all the sureties.

    (ii) Under Justinian a surety had the right of *beneficium ordinis* by which the creditor was obliged to claim in the first place from the principal debtor.

(c) *To create agency* (*e.g.* a principal gives his agent a mandate to buy property from a third party). In general the agent was always personally liable on a contract. In certain cases the Praetor allowed *actiones adjecticiae qualitatis* under which it was possible to sue the principal directly.

    (i) Where the principal had authorised or ratified the contract of his slave or son in *potestas*, an *actio quod jussu* could be brought against him.

    (ii) Where the principal was a shipowner and his son or slave was employed as the ship's captain, an *actio exercitoria* could be brought against him for contracts concerning the ship.

    (iii) Where the principal owned a business and his son or slave managed that business the *actio institoria* could be brought against him for debts incurred in carrying on the business.

    (iv) Where a son or slave had traded by using his *peculium* (*see* V, **4**), an *actio de peculio* could be brought against the *paterfamilias* or the master.

    (v) Where a son or slave had traded with his *peculium* with the knowledge of the *paterfamilias* or master, an *actio tributoria* could be brought against the *paterfamilias* or master requiring the *pro rata* distribution of the *peculium* between them and the creditors.

PROGRESS TEST 17

1. What were the four consensual contracts? **(2)**

2. "The *res* sold had to be *specific*." Explain. **(4)**

3. Explain (a) *emptio rei speratae,* (b) *emptio spei.* **(4)**

4. On what grounds might a contract of sale have been set aside because of an unreasonable price? **(4)**

5. Outline the duties of the *venditor.* **(6)**

6. What was meant by (a) *pactum displicentiae,* (b) *emptio ad gustum*? **(7)**

7. Define *locatio conductio.* **(9)**

8. What were the duties of the *locator*? (10)

9. In what circumstances could a contract of *locatio conductio* be determined? (12)

10. Explain the nature of *societas*. (14)

11. What was the difference between *societas universorum bonorum* and *societas universorum bonorum quae ex quaestu veniunt*? (15)

12. Explain how *societas* might be determined (a) *ex rebus*, (b) *ex voluntate*. (17)

13. Define *mandatum*. What types of mandate could exist? (19, 20)

14. Outline the duties of the *mandatarius*. (21)

15. Under what circumstances could a mandate be determined? (23)

16. How could a mandate be used to create agency? (25)

CHAPTER XVIII

CONTRACTS—3: INNOMINATE CONTRACTS, PACTS AND QUASI-CONTRACT

INNOMINATE CONTRACTS

1. General. Innominate (nameless) contracts were agreements which did not fall within the recognised forms of contracts, but which were enforceable where one party had performed that which he had promised to do, *i.e.* they were contracts arising out of part performance.

> EXAMPLE: Aulus agrees to give Balbus a silver cup in exchange for a golden brooch. If Aulus gives the cup, and Balbus then refuses to give the brooch to Aulus, Aulus may claim damages or the restoration of his property.

2. Examples of Innominate Contracts.

(a) *Permutatio* (*exchange*). See the example above. Agreements to exchange gave rise to obligations only when one party had carried out his part of the transaction. The property passed on delivery and before performance by the other party (*see* also **12** below).

(b) *Aestimatum* (*contract for sale or return*). An article is given by X to Y so that Y might sell it and pay a fixed sum to X. In the event of Y's failing to sell, the article has to be restored to X.

(c) *Precarium* (*permissive occupancy*). This arose where X was allowed the tenancy of land or a servitude (*see* XI, **4**) only so long as Y, the owner, pleased. X was obliged to surrender possession on demand and was liable for damage done to the property whilst in his possession. X's death, but not necessarily Y's, ended the tenancy. Possession with the owner's consent sufficed for the creation of the tenancy.

3. Actions. The *actio praescriptis verbis* was available to either party. In *aestimatum* the *actio de aestimatio* was also available. In the case of *precarium*, the owner's rights could be enforced by the interdict *de precario*.

PACTS

4. General. Pacts were simple agreements which fell neither within the category of nominate nor innominate contracts, but which could be enforced under certain circumstances. Pacts were either:

(a) *Pacta Vestita* ("clothed" pacts), or
(b) *Pacta Nuda* ("bare" pacts).

5. Pacta Vestita (pacts clothed with obligation). Certain pacts were made the basis of actions, hence they were given the force of contractual agreements, although they were not contracts in the strict sense. The three types of *pacta vestita* were:

(a) *Pacta legitima* (*see* **6** below).
(b) *Pacta adjecta* (*see* **7** below).
(c) *Pacta praetoria* (*see* **8** below).

6. Pacta legitima. These were pacts which had been made actionable as the result of imperial legislation, *e.g.*

(a) Agreements to refer matters to arbitration.
(b) Informal agreements to give *dos* (*see* VI, **26**), which were made actionable under Theodosius and Valentinian in A.D. **428**.

7. Pacta adjecta. These were pacts added to a main contract. They could be sued on if made contemporaneously with the contract (*pacta continua*); if made subsequent to the main contract (*pacta ex intervallo*) they could not be sued on, but might be available as a defence.

8. Pacta praetoria. The Praetors recognised certain pacts as binding. Examples of this type of pact were:

(a) *Constitutum debiti.* This was an informal promise to pay an existing debt at an agreed time.

> EXAMPLE: Brutus owes Cassius 50 *aurei*, on a contract of *mutuum* (*see* XVI, **3**), to be paid by a particular date. Brutus fails to pay on that date and is allowed by Cassius a further month in which to pay. The agreement allowing a further month is a *constitutum*. If Cassius should

successfully sue on this *constitutum* he could obtain the original debt plus one half, as a penalty.

(b) *Receptum argentariorum* (*argentarius* = a banker). In this case a banker has in his possession property of a customer and agrees informally to discharge the obligations of that customer.

(c) *Receptum arbitri*. Where parties had come to an agreement to submit a dispute to arbitration, the arbitrator who had agreed to make the award could be compelled to act by the Praetor.

(d) *Receptum nautarum, stabulariorum, cauponum*. Masters of ships, stablekeepers and innkeepers were liable, by Praetorian edict (except in the case of *vis major*, *e.g.* earthquake), for the safety of goods placed on their premises or ships (*see* also **XX, 4**).

9. Actions. The *actio de pecunia constituta* was available on a *constitutum debiti*. The creditor had an *actio recepticia* in the case of *receptum argentariorum*. An *actio de recepto* could be brought on the *receptum nautarum, stabulariorum, cauponum*.

OBLIGATIONES QUASI EX CONTRACTU

10. Their nature. Quasi-contractual obligations were those which were imposed by law on equitable grounds or because of public policy, and which did not arise from any agreement of the parties. Examples are given in **11–14** below.

11. Indebiti solutio. Where X paid money to Y under a mistake of fact an obligation on Y to repay the money arose. No similar obligation arose where the payment had been made under a mistake of law. The relevant actions were the *condictio indebiti* or the *condictio incerti*.

12. Condictio causa data causa non secuta (*purpose stated but not realised*). Where X hands property to Y for a particular purpose and that purpose fails, X could recover the property, or its value, *e.g.* where money was given as *dos* and the marriage did not take place.

13. Condictio ob turpem causam, ob injustam causam. Where money was received for an illegal or immoral purpose,

THE LAW OF OBLIGATIONS

or as the result of an illegal or immoral action, it could be recovered if the receiver alone was the *turpis persona* (wrongdoer).

14. Negotiorum gestio (*the "management of affairs"*). An obligation arose where one party (*negotiorum gestor*) rendered services to another without a mandate or other obligation to do so. It was essential that he should not have been forbidden to render this particular service. The *negotiorum gestor* was bound to exercise *exacta diligentia* (*see* XVI, **11** (c)) and he had to account to the person for whom the services were rendered. He was liable for *dolus* (intentionally wrongful acts), but not for negligence or accidents. The principal (*dominus rei gestae*) for whom the services were rendered had to pay expenses incurred by the *negotiorum gestor* on his behalf.

EXAMPLE: While Marcus is away on military service, his neighbour, Ligarius, observes that a wall of Marcus's house is crumbling. Ligarius buys bricks and mortar and repairs the wall. Ligarius has acted in the capacity of *negotiorum gestor* and can claim his expenditure from Ligarius.

The *dominus* had an *actio negotiorum gestorum* against the *gestor*; the *gestor* had an *actio negotiorum contraria* against the *dominus*.

PROGRESS TEST 18

1. What was an innominate contract? **(1)**
2. Explain (a) *permutatio*, (b) *precarium*. **(2)**
3. Illustrate the difference between *pacta vestita* and *pacta nuda*. **(4, 5)**
4. Give examples of *pacta legitima*. **(6)**
5. Explain the *constitutum debiti*. **(8)**
6. What was meant by *obligationes quasi ex contractu*? **(10)**
7. Explain (a) *indebiti solutio*, (b) *condictio causa data causa non secuta*. **(11, 12)**
8. Discuss the legal principle involved in the following case: Gaius leaves his house in Rome for a holiday in the provinces. A week after he has left, a neighbour, Clitus, observes that hooligans are battering down the ornamental doors of Gaius's house. Clitus chases them away and, at his own expense, repairs the doors. Gaius returns a week later. He refuses to compensate Clitus for the expenses of the repairs. **(14)**

Obligationes ex delicto and quasi ex delicto

Delicts (XIX)

Injuria (3–5)

Damnum Injuria Datum (6–10)

Furtum (11–15)

Rapina (16–19)

Praetorian Delicts (20–23)

Servi Corruptio (21)

Dolus (22)

Metus (23)

Quasi-Delicts (XX)

Dejectum vel Effusum (2)

Positum vel Suspensum (3)

Edict Nautae, etc. (4)

Judex qui Litem suam fecerit (5)

CHAPTER XIX

DELICTS

THE NATURE OF DELICTS

1. General. Public crimes (*crimina publica*), which involved offences against the public were covered by the criminal law and led to public criminal proceedings. Wrongs perpetrated against a person, or his family, or his property (*delicta privata*) were the concern of private law. From *delicta privata* arose obligations to make reparations. Four important delicts treated in the Institutes are:

(a) *Injuria* (the violation of a freeman's rights in respect of his own person) (*see* **3–5** below).
(b) *Damnum Injuria Datum* (damage of property and the injuring of its usefulness) (*see* **6–10** below).
(c) *Furtum* (theft) (*see* **11–15** below).
(d) *Rapina* (robbery) (*see* **16–19** below).

2. Characteristics of delicts and delictual actions.

(a) A delict involved an intentional or wrongful act or omission.
(b) The wrong had to be of such a nature that, under the early law, some kind of vengeance would have been permitted.
(c) The delictual actions were of a penal nature (*actiones poenales*).
(d) Where two or more persons committed a delict, each of them was liable separately for the entire amount, and satisfaction by one wrongdoer did not act to release the others; hence an injured person was able to obtain full compensation from each one of the wrongdoers.

INJURIA

3. Definition. The wilful and unjustifiable violation of the rights of a freeman to freedom, safety and reputation.

EXAMPLES
  (i) Casca strikes Trebonius without just cause.
 (ii) Casca enters the house of Trebonius against Trebonius's will.
(iii) Casca defames Trebonius by publishing a scurrilous poem about him.

4. Penalties.

(a) *Under the XII Tables.* A broken bone—300 *asses* where the injured person was a freeman; in the case of a slave, his owner could claim 150 *asses*. A broken limb—retaliation, unless the parties agreed on terms of compensation. Other types of injury—25 *asses*.
(b) *Praetorian penalty.* The Praetor introduced the *actio injuriarum*, by which plaintiff made an estimate of the damages and the judge was given the power of modification if he considered the sum unreasonable. The action could not be brought after one year, nor could it be transmitted to plaintiff's heir. It was not available where the harm complained of was the result of negligence only, nor where defendant had acted in self-defence. Where more than one person was affected by the wrongful act, each person could bring a separate action.

5. Injuria atrox (aggravated insult).

Where a wrong was committed in circumstances which led to its being especially outrageous, heavy damages could be awarded. Such a wrong might be committed:

(a) By reason of the rank of the person injured (*ex persona*), *e.g.* a senator.
(b) Because of the nature of the act (*ex facto*), *e.g.* a beating with a heavy stick.
(c) By reason of the public nature of the place in which it was committed (*ex loco*), *e.g.* in a public theatre.
(d) Because of the special vulnerability of the part of the body which was injured (*ex loco vulneris*), *e.g.* a blow in the eye.

DAMNUM INJURIA DATUM

6. Definition.

A statutory delict created by the *Lex Aquilia* (*see* **8** below) involving wrongful damage to property and thereby causing a pecuniary loss.

EXAMPLES
  (i) Sempronius wilfully kills cattle belonging to Brutus.
  (ii) Septimius wilfully throws a stone at Brutus's horse and breaks its leg.

7. Remedies under the old law. Under the XII Tables remedies were provided for injuries such as maiming, breaking bones, burning a building, secretly cutting down trees, causing damage by allowing trespass of cattle, etc.

8. Lex Aquilia (c. 286 B.C.).

(a) The date of this *plebiscitum* (*see* II, **16**) is not certain. It is known to have been carried by Aquilius, a Tribune of the Plebs, during the course of the struggle between the plebeians and the patricians.

(b) *The Lex enacted:*

  (i) *By c.I*, that any person who wrongfully killed a slave, or a four-footed creature coming under the description of "cattle," belonging to another person was liable to the owner in damage equal to the highest value which the thing slain had possessed during the previous year.

  (ii) *By c.II*, that an *adstipulator* (*see* XVI, **33**) who released a debtor with the intention of defrauding the principal stipulator was liable for the loss so caused. (This had become obsolete by Justinian's time.)

  (iii) *By c.III*, that a person who damaged property, other than by killing a slave or a four-footed animal (as in *c.I* above), by breaking, burning or destroying, was liable to the owner in damages based on the highest value the damaged property possessed during the preceding thirty days.

  NOTE: A person who denied his liability under the *Lex* and was subsequently condemned, was obliged to pay double damages.

  EXAMPLES
  (i) Gaius wrongfully beats and kills Seius, the slave of Aulus. In a subsequent action under *Lex Aquilia*, Gaius denies his liability. Aulus establishes that the highest value of a slave such as Seius during the previous year was 50 *aurei*. Gaius is condemned and, as a result of his denial of liability, may have to pay damages of 100 *aurei*.
  (ii) Marcus wrongfully burns a barn containing grain belonging to Cassius. Under the *Lex* he would be

liable to Cassius for the highest value of the property destroyed during the thirty days preceding
the burning.

9. Liability under Lex Aquilia. Liability under the *Lex* was
incurred when there was an intentional or negligent act which
was wrongful, and which resulted in damage being suffered by
the owner of the property which had been injured.

(a) *Intentional or wrongful act.* A positive act was generally
essential. An omission would not create liability in itself
under the *Lex*, but where, for example, a person had undertaken to perform a task, that task had to be concluded
properly. A dentist who extracted a slave's teeth could be
held liable for injury resulting to the slave arising out of
failure to administer correct treatment immediately following the extraction. No liability arose because of acci-
dent (in the absence of negligence) or where damage was
caused by the contributory negligence of the person injured. Want of skill was construed as negligence; hence,
an unskilful doctor might be liable under the *Lex* for
damage resulting from his lack of skill.

> NOTE: Because intention could not be imputed to very
> young children or to the insane, they were not considered
> to be liable under the *Lex Aquilia*.

(b) *Wrongful.* There must be neither excuse nor lawful justi-
fication, *e.g.* damage caused as the result of self-defence.
(c) *Damage being suffered by the owner.* Pecuniary loss had to
arise out of the wrongful act. Where there was no pecuniary loss, there was no action under the *Lex*.

10. Extensions of the scope of Lex Aquilia. The Praetor ex-
tended the scope of the *Lex* by allowing the *actio utilis quasi ex
Legis Aquiliae* (an action adapted from, and based on, *Lex
Aquilia*). This extension affected three matters:

(a) *Persons who could bring the action.* Under the *Lex* an action
by the *dominus* (master) only was allowed. Through
actions *in factum* and *utiles* its remedies were made available
to pledgees, usufructuaries and usuaries, *bona fide* posses-
sors, and *coloni* (for damage to crops).
(b) *Wrongful acts for which a remedy was available.* The *Lex*
applied only to the direct killing of a slave or four-footed

animal, or to direct damage caused *corpore corpori* ("by body to body"). The extension covered a case where death was the direct consequence of an act, even though no direct contact *corpore corpori* had taken place, as, for example, where X intentionally drops a heavy stone on a horse's head, as a result of which the horse is killed. Acts of spoiling or destruction were also included. Indirect killing, as where A intentionally jostles B, who pushes C, as a result of which C is killed, gave rise to an *actio in factum*. An action was available also in the case of indirect infliction of loss, *e.g.* where X knocks a gold ornament from Y's hands and it is lost in a stream into which it falls; or where injury, but not death, was inflicted on a freeman.

(c) *The measure of damages.* The *Lex* calculated damages based on the actual value of the object. *Interpretatio* of the jurists (*see* II, **19**) allowed the inclusion in damages of:

  (i) *Lucrum cessans*, *i.e.* gain which might have accrued.
     EXAMPLE: Stichus, slave of Aulus, has been instituted heir to Balbus's estate, which is worth 200 *aurei*. Stichus is unlawfully killed. Aulus's estimate of damages will include the value of Stichus, plus 200 *aurei*.

  (ii) *Damnum emergens*, *i.e.* loss due to extrinsic circumstances.
     EXAMPLE: Marcus is one of a company of slave musicians belonging to Flavius and is unlawfully killed. Flavius could include in his estimate of damages not only the value of Marcus, but also any consequent decrease in value of the company of musicians.

FURTUM

11. Definition. "The dishonest handling of a thing with a view to gain either of the thing itself or of the use or possession of it." (*The Digest*)

(a) *Dishonest handling.* An intention to steal the thing is essential. The thief must be aware that he has not got the owner's consent to the act. Handling does not necessarily imply carrying away.

(b) *A thing.* This particular delict concerns only movables in someone's ownership. (This would include slaves and free persons in *potestas* (*see* V).)

(c) *Use.* Where a borrower, for example, misused that which had been lent to him, he was considered to have stolen the use of that thing (*furtum usus*).

(d) *Possession.* Where an owner, for example, retakes by fraudulent means some thing given by him in pledge, he is considered to have stolen its possession (*furtum possessionis*).

12. Types of furtum.

(a) *Furtum Manifestum* (*theft in the hand*). Where a thief was caught in the act of stealing, or before leaving the place of theft, he was held to have committed *furtum manifestum*. Justinian extended this to include the case of a thief apprehended on the day of the theft, in possession of the stolen goods, before reaching the place where he had intended to deposit them.

(b) *Furtum Nec Manifestum* (*theft not in the hand*). Where a thief was caught in conditions other than those described in (a) above.

13. Penalties and Actions. These will be considered as they occurred in the early law, as a result of praetorian development, and in the time of Justinian.

(a) *By the XII Tables.*

    (i) *The actio furti.* *Furtum manifestum* was a capital offence. A guilty slave could be killed; a freeman could be reduced to slavery. *Furtum nec manifestum* involved double damages.

    (ii) *The actio furti oblati.* Threefold damages could be awarded against X who had passed stolen property to Y, with the intention that it should be found on Y's premises. In such a case Y could bring the action.

    (iii) *The actio furti concepti.* Damages were awarded against a receiver in whose premises stolen goods were discovered. Treble damages were awarded in the very early law, and fourfold damages by the XII Tables, in the case of stolen goods found on premises as the result of a formal search.

(b) *Praetorian Remedies.*

    (i) *Actio furti manifesti.* Fourfold damages awarded against the thief.

    (ii) *Actio furti nec manifesti.* Twofold damages awarded against the thief.

(iii) *Actio furti non exhibiti.* Damages (unknown) were awarded against a person on his refusal to produce stolen property discovered on his premises.

(iv) *Actio furti prohibiti.* Fourfold damages were awarded against a person who resisted a search for stolen property on his premises.

(c) *At the time of Justinian.*

  (i) *Actio furti manifesti*
  (ii) *Actio furti nec manifesti* } as (b)(i) and (ii), above.

(iii) *Condictio furtiva.* This action could be brought by the owner of goods against the thief, or against the thief's heir. Recovery of the goods, or their value, could be demanded.

(iv) *Actio ad exhibendum.* Available against any person alleged to be in possession of the stolen goods, to secure their production in court. The action could be brought by any person entitled to possession.

  (v) *Rei vindicatio.* Available to the owner against a person in possession of the stolen goods for their recovery.

(vi) *Actio rerum amotarum.* Available against a spouse who had stolen the other's property in contemplation of a divorce which followed the stealing.

14. Aiders and abettors. The *actio furti* could be brought not only against the thief, but against any person who aided and advised the thief (*ope et consilio*). Active assistance was necessary; advice and encouragement alone did not suffice.

EXAMPLE: Aulus ties a rope ladder to the window of Marcus' house so that Balbus is able to enter and steal a silver brooch. Stichus stands near the ladder whispering encouragement to Balbus. The *actio furti* could be brought against Aulus and Balbus, but not against Stichus.

15. Availability of the actio furti. In general the action was available not only to the owner, but to all persons who had an interest in the safety of the property stolen. Each person was able to sue the thief to the extent of his particular interest. Thus, the action was available to a pledgee.

RAPINA

16. Definition. Theft accompanied by force, *i.e.* robbery.

17. Origin. Robbery was treated originally as mere theft.

The Social War (91–89 B.C.) gave rise to a great increase in the number of crimes of violence, and in 76 B.C. the Praetor Lucullus established *rapina* as a separate delict.

18. Actions and Penalties. The *actio vi bonorum raptorum* was available to anyone with a legal interest in the property. Thus the action could be brought by a person who had merely detention of goods and not their possession (*see* X, 1). Where the action was brought within one year of the robbery fourfold damages (which included the value of the stolen property) could be claimed. Where the action was brought after one year (*annus utilis*) only the value of the stolen property could be claimed.

19. Constitution of Valentinian, Theodosius and Arcadius (A.D. 389). Under this enactment, a person who took by force movable property which belonged to him would forfeit that property. Where a person took by force property under the mistaken impression that it belonged to him, he was obliged to restore it to the owner and pay its value.

EXAMPLE: Marcus sees a horse in Casca's team and, under the impression that the horse belongs to him, seizes it by force from Casca. The horse, in fact, belongs to Casca. Marcus would have to restore the horse to Casca and pay its value.

PRAETORIAN DELICTS

20. General. The Praetors classified a number of wrongful actions as delicts. Three of these so-called Praetorian Delicts were:

Servi Corruptio (corruption of a slave); *Dolus* (fraud, deceit); *Metus* (duress).

21. Servi Corruptio. To act against a slave so as to bring about his moral or physical deterioration could give rise to a suit based on the *actio servi corrupti*. The action was not extinguished by the manumission or death of the slave.

22. Dolus. This involved a deception by D perpetrated with the intention of obtaining an unfair advantage over P and resulting in loss to P. The *actio doli* (introduced by the Praetor Gallus), or *restitutio in integrum* (*see* XXIII, **17**), was available to P. *Dolus* could arise, for example, in the case of a contract between P and D in which D deceives P as to the subject matter of the agreement.

23. Metus. This arose in the case of a transaction into which P enters as the result of intimidation by D. Such a transaction could be set aside before completion. The intimidation had to consist of threats of bodily injury, enslavement or death to P or members of P's family. Should the transaction have been completed P could ask for *restitutio in integrum*, or an *actio quod metus causa* which could result in fourfold damages.

PROGRESS TEST 19

1. Define delict. **(1)**
2. What were the important characteristics of a delict? **(2)**
3. Name four delicts and give an example of each. **(1)**
4. Identify the delicts arising in the following cases:
   (a) Marcus wilfully hurls a javelin at a sheep belonging to Quintus and kills it; **(6)**
   (b) Seius knocks Balbus to the ground, seizes his purse and runs off with it. **(16)**
5. What were the penalties under the XII Tables for *injuria*? **(4)**
6. What was the *actio injuriarum*? **(4)**
7. To whom was a right of action available in the case of *injuria* done to a wife? **(4)**
8. Give two examples of *injuria atrox*. **(5)**
9. What were the provisions of *c.I* and *c.III* of *Lex Aquilia*? **(8)**
10. How were the provisions of *Lex Aquilia* extended by the Praetor and the Jurists? **(10)**
11. Define *furtum*. **(11)**
12. Distinguish *furtum manifestum* and *furtum nec manifestum*. **(12)**
13. Explain (a) *condictio furtiva*, (b) *actio furti non exhibiti*. **(13)**
14. What is meant by "stealing the use" of a thing? **(11)**
15. Name and illustrate any two praetorian delicts. **(20)**
16. Consider the legal position in the following cases:
    (a) Marcus steals a golden trumpet from Cassius. He hides it in the house of Balbus, where it is found. **(13)**
    (b) Balbus stands in the entrance to a theatre and, in the presence of a large crowd, shouts abuse at Gaius, an important senator. **(5)**
    (c) Maevius gives property in pledge to Titinius. The next day Maevius enters the house of Titinius without permission and removes the property. **(11)**

CHAPTER XX

QUASI-DELICTS AND NOXAL SURRENDER

QUASI-DELICTS

1. General. The Institutes discuss four specific cases of obligations arising *quasi ex delicto*. The four wrongs (*see* 2–5 below) were made actionable by edict; they did not come within the general category of delicts since they involved an element of vicarious responsibility or did not fall within the terms of a statute. The four quasi-delicts were:

    (a) *Dejectum vel effusum* (**2** below).
    (b) *Positum vel suspensum* (**3** below).
    (c) *Edict Nautae, Caupones, Stabularii* (**4** below).
    (d) *Judex qui Litem suam fecerit* (**5** below).

2. Dejectum vel effusum. Where injury was caused by anything thrown or poured from a window or a house by any person upon a commonly frequented place, the occupier of the house was responsible in double damages for any loss so caused. The appropriate action was the *actio de effusis vel ejectis*. The injury of a freeman brought liability for damages in a sum which could be fixed at the judge's discretion. In this case the action was available only as long as the injured man was alive; it did not pass to his heirs. The killing of a freeman brought a penalty of 50 *solidi*; in this case any person (preferably a near relative) might sue (*see* XXII, **7**).

NOTE
    (i) If more than one person was liable, satisfaction by one freed the others.
    (ii) The occupier of the house could bring an action *in factum* so as to reimburse himself against the actual wrongdoer.

3. Positum vel suspensum. The *actio de positis vel suspensis* could be brought by any person against the occupier of a house from which there was suspended over a public way any thing likely to cause damage to persons passing by. A penalty of 10 *solidi* could be imposed, even though no actual damage had been caused. Where damage was caused it was considered as under 2 above.

4. Edict Nautae, Caupones, Stabularii.

Where damage was caused by the fraud or theft of servants of shipowners, innkeepers or stable keepers, the servants' masters were held responsible. An *actio in factum* was available for double damages against a master. An innkeeper was also held responsible for similar acts committed by his residents. Note an alternative procedure mentioned in XVIII, 8(d).

5. Judex qui Litem suam fecerit. (The judge who "makes the case his own.")

In early law a judge who accepted a bribe was liable to be condemned to death. Under Augustus very heavy penalties were enacted for this offence. An obligation *quasi ex delicto* was considered to arise where a judge gave a decision which was corrupt, or beyond his terms of reference, or based on ignorance of the law. In these circumstances an *actio in factum* could be brought against the judge, who was liable for any loss caused by his decision.

NOXAL SURRENDER

6. Its meaning.

The term *noxae deditio* (noxal surrender) refers to the handing over to a wronged person the cause of the wrong or mischief (*noxa* = injury). Noxal liability followed the person of the wrongdoer (*noxa caput sequitur*).

EXAMPLES
  (i) Sempronius, slave of Titius, commits a wrong and is later sold to Marcus. If the wrong was one which could bring a noxal surrender, a noxal action could be brought against Marcus.
  (ii) Brutus, son of Flavius and in his power, commits a wrong which could bring noxal surrender. He is later given in adoption to Aulus (*see* V, 8). In this case a noxal action could be brought against Aulus.

The alternative to noxal surrender was the payment of damages. Noxal liability arose, for example, from *furtum* (*see* XIX, 11) and from *damnum injuria datum* (*see* XIX, 6).

NOTE: Where a slave who had committed a wrong was sold to the injured person so that he passed into his ownership, the noxal action was extinguished.

7. Noxal Surrender of Persons.

(a) *Slaves.* A slave handed over in noxal surrender became the property of the transferee. He could demand that the transferee free him after he had compensated for the damage for which he had been responsible.

(b) *Sons.* A son entered the *mancipium* (bondage) of the transferee. When he had compensated the transferee by his labour he was entitled to emancipation. Justinian abolished the noxal surrender of sons.

8. Noxal Surrender of Animals.

(a) *Under the XII Tables.* The noxal *actio de pauperie* was available against the owner of a quadruped which, in the absence of provocation or external cause had caused damage by acting contrary to its usual nature. Penalties might be avoided by a surrender of the offending animal. The action did not apply in the case of an animal savage by nature, *e.g.* a lion. The *actio de pastu pecoris* was available for damage caused by cattle allowed by their owner to pasture on another person's property.

(b) *By Aedilician Edict.* Noxal surrender did not apply in the case of an animal kept near a public highway and liable, by its nature, to cause damage, *e.g.* a wild boar. Where such an animal caused injury to a freeman, the owner was liable in damages assessed at the judge's discretion. Where the freeman was killed there was a penalty of 200 *solidi*. Twofold damages could be claimed in other cases of injury.

PROGRESS TEST 20

1. What is meant by quasi-delict? **(1)**
2. Under what circumstances could the *actio de effusis vel ejectis* be brought? **(2)**
3. Consider the legal position in the following case:
   Stichus owns an inn and employs Publius to look after the stables. Seius stays at the inn for a night, during which his horse is wilfully injured by Publius. Before leaving, Seius

discovers that his brooch has been stolen. The brooch is found in the possession of Marcus, a resident at the inn. **(4)**

4. What was involved in the noxal surrender of a slave? **(6, 7)**

5. Examine the legal principles in the following case:
A dog, kept as a household pet by Brutus, is stung by a wasp. The dog is irritated and bites Veratius, who is visiting Brutus. **(8)**

PART SIX

THE LAW OF ACTIONS

CHAPTER XXI

THE LEGIS ACTIONES PROCEDURE

THE LAW OF ACTIONS

1. General. The Law of Actions concerned itself with remedies and procedures; remedies involving the trial of a dispute before a judge, and procedures applicable to particular forms of action. The processes of an action will be separated for consideration as follows:

(a) events preceding the trial, *i.e.* the summons and the methods whereby the defendant is brought before the court;
(b) the trial;
(c) events following the trial, *i.e.* methods by which the judgment is executed.

2. The Three Modes of Procedure.

(a) *Legis Actiones Procedure* (*considered in this chapter*). This procedure, normally available to Roman citizens only, was a feature of the ancient *jus civile* and was characterised by a rigid adherence to form (*see* **3–4** below) and by proceedings *in jure* and *in judicio* (*see* **6–9** below).
(b) *The Formulary System* (see **XXII**). This procedure superseded *legis actiones* and was characterised by formulae (*see* **XXII, 18–23**) which stated the nature of plaintiff's claim.
(c) *The Cognitio Extraordinaria* (*see* **XXIII**). In the last years of the Principate the formulary system was superseded by a procedure under which the trial was conducted in a single hearing.

LEGIS ACTIONES

3. The nature of legis actiones procedure. The essence of the *legis actiones* (= actions of the law) was a series of solemn and formal acts, any error in which could result in dismissal of the action. Each wrong had its own appropriate *legis actio*. Proceedings consisted of two hearings:

(a) *in jure* (before the magistrate), and
(b) *in judicio* (before a private citizen acting as a judge). The parties to the action had to participate personally in the formalities and could not be represented by a procurator or an agent.

4. Decline of the legis actiones procedure. The reasons for this decline were:

(a) The excessive technicalities of the procedure and the rigid rules of interpretation meant that the procedure failed to answer the needs of an expanding community.
(b) The procedure was not available for the many aliens living in Rome.
(c) The necessity for the presence in court of parties and the inability to be represented by an agent became cumbrous.

Lex Aebutia (c. 120 B.C.), which sanctioned the use of formulae, hastened the decline of a procedure of which it has been said: "Form was everything and substantial justice nothing."

EVENTS PRECEDING THE TRIAL

5. The Summons (in jus vocatio). Under the early law plaintiff had the task of bringing defendant before the court. By the XII Tables a plaintiff was instructed to act thus:

"If one shall summon a man to court, let him go: if he does not go, call a witness to this; then take him. If he should evade or flee, then lay hands upon him."

Defendant, after being summoned to court, was allowed to give security (*vadimonium*) for his appearance before the magistrate.

THE TRIAL

6. Proceedings in jure and in judicio.

(a) Proceedings *in jure* were designed to establish the precise question which was to be settled *in judicio*.

(b) In the first stage of the proceedings, the magistrate had to decide whether, if plaintiff's statements were assumed to be correct, plaintiff would have a right which could be legally enforced. If he so found, he granted plaintiff an action (*actionem dat*); if he found no basis for a civil action, he refused it (*actionem denegat*).

(c) In the second stage, a private judge (*see* note below) heard evidence and delivered judgment.

> NOTE: A private judge (*judex*) was not a magistrate, but merely a private Roman citizen who was invested with a judicial commission for a particular case. In early law he was selected from the Senators, but, at a later date, an official list of judges was compiled. In the time of Augustus, for example, there were 4,000 *judices* (*see* also XXII, **14**(a)).

c) The types of *legis actiones* considered below formed the framework of the solemn procedure by which a trial was commenced, or by which the execution of a judgment might be initiated.

7. Legis Actio Sacramento (sacramentum = a wager). Plaintiff and defendant staked a fixed amount of money (*summa sacramenti*). The judgment decided which of the wagers was just; the stake deposited by the loser went to the Treasury. Gaius (*see* III, **15**) states that the amount of the *sacramentum* varied according to the value of the matter in dispute: 500 *asses* where the subject matter was valued at over 1,000 *asses*; 50 *asses* where its value was less than 1,000 *asses*, or in proceedings involving a person's liberty.

(a) *Legis actio sacramento in rem.* Where proceedings were *in rem* (*see* XI, **1**) arising, for example, out of *patria potestas*, or ownership of slaves, and the *res* in question was movable property which could be produced in court, the following ritual of events took place:

> (i) Plaintiff (P) and defendant (D) come before the magistrate carrying a symbolic representation of quiritary ownership (*see* X, **2**), usually a rod.
>
> (ii) P grasps the *res*—in this case, a slave—and claims him by using a set mode of words and touching the slave with his rod. D repeats the words, after which the magistrate orders, "Both let the man go!"
>
> (iii) P then asks D why he has claimed the *res* and D answers, "I told my right as I laid on my rod."

    (iv) P then challenges D to a wager and D challenges P.

    (v) P and D make their wager on oath.

    (vi) The magistrate awards the *res* to P or D, pending settlement of the dispute by a *judex*. Security for restoration of the *res* is then obtained.

    (vii) A *judex* is nominated and the case goes to him.

    (viii) P and D appear before the *judex* to state their case and to produce evidence on the third day following nomination of the *judex*.

    (ix) The *judex* decides the issue and pronounces judgment declaring the *sacramentum* of P or D to be *injustum*.

> NOTE: Where the *res* was immovable a part of it was produced symbolically in court, *e.g.* a turf to represent land, a tile to represent a building.

(b) *Legis Actio Sacramento in personam.* Little is known of the details of this procedure. It is assumed that (iv)–(ix) above were preceded by P's asserting D's liability and requesting D to admit or deny liability.

8. Legis Actio per Judicis Arbitrive Postulationem. This procedure was available only for actions *in personam* and involved a request to the Praetor for the appointment of a *judex* or *arbiter*. P recited his formula, "I assert that by your promise you should give me 100 *sesterces*. Do you admit or deny this?" D denied, upon which P said, "Because you deny, I ask you, Praetor, to give a *judex* or *arbiter*." No *sacramentum* was involved.

9. Legis Actio per Condictionem. No *sacramentum* was used in this mode of procedure. P stated, "I assert that you should give me 100 *sesterces*. I ask you, do you admit or deny?" Upon D's denial, P stated, "Because you deny, I give you notice for the thirtieth day to have a judge appointed." An adjournment of thirty days was the characteristic of this action which seems to have been used only in claims for fixed amounts of money.

EVENTS FOLLOWING THE TRIAL

10. Legis Actio per Manus Injectionem. In the case of a successful action *in personam*, execution could be made, after thirty days, on the body of the debtor. The successful plaintiff seized the debtor and, after reciting a set style of words, was held to have obtained power over the body of the debtor.

In early times, if the debt had not been satisfied within a further sixty days, enslavement or death of the debtor followed (*see* XV, **17**). This mode of execution was applicable only to a case in which liability had been determined in monetary terms; where this had not been done an assessment had to be made by arbitration (*arbitrium litis aestimandae*).

A debtor who wished to escape the consequences of *manus injectio* was obliged to satisfy the judgment or to obtain the help of a *vindex* (a person who would act as security), who would attempt in a subsequent action to obtain a reversal of the judgment—with a penalty of twofold damages in the event of failure.

NOTE: A *proletarius* (person lacking landed property) was prohibited from acting as *vindex* for an *adsiduus* (landowner).

11. Use of Manus Injectio procedure. *Manus injectio* seems to have been used in particular:

(a) in actions arising on debts contracted with a pledge of the debtor's body as security;
(b) in judgment debts;
(c) in the case of a defendant's refusal to obey a summons requiring him to appear before a magistrate;
(d) under *Lex Publilia* (fourth or third century B.C.) against a principal debtor by a sponsor who had paid a debt and had not been reimbursed within six months;
(e) under *Lex Furia de sponsu* (*c.* 195 B.C.) against a creditor who had taken more than his *pro rata* share from one of several sponsors.

12. Manus Injectio Pura. A form of *manus injectio* of a less severe character was introduced under the later law. Under this mode of procedure the debtor could resist arrest and defend himself in a subsequent action without a *vindex* (*see* **10** above). Following *Lex Vallia* (*c.* 200 B.C.) *manus injectio* in all cases except 11 (*b*) and (*d*) above became *pura*.

13. Legis Actio per Pignoris Capionem. In a few cases, arising largely out of custom, creditors could distrain (*i.e.* seize goods) in satisfaction of, or as security for, a debt due and unpaid. Examples of these cases were:

(a) A soldier, who could distrain upon his paymaster for his

pay (*aes militare*), so as to buy a horse (*aes equestre*) or to buy forage for it (*aes hordearium*).
(b) By the XII Tables distress could be levied by the seller of an animal for sacrificial purposes against the purchaser who had failed to pay the agreed price.
(c) *Publicani* (farmers of taxes) could levy distress against those whose taxes were in arrear.

NOTE
(i) *Legis actio per pignoris capionem* required, as in the case of other *legis actiones*, a set style of words spoken in the presence of witnesses.
(ii) For Appeals *see* XXIII.

PROGRESS TEST 21

1. What was the essential nature of *legis actiones* procedure? **(3)**
2. Account for the decline in *legis actiones* procedure. **(4)**
3. Explain the nature of *in jus vocatio* under the early law. **(5)**
4. Outline the proceeding *in jure* and *in judicio*. **(6)**
5. Explain *legis actio sacramento in rem*. **(7)**
6. What was *legis actio per judicis arbitrive postulationem*? **(8)**
7. Outline *legis actio per manus injectionem*. **(10)**
8. What was *manus injectio pura*? **(12)**
9. Give an account of *legis actio per pignoris capionem*. **(13)**

CHAPTER XXII

THE FORMULARY SYSTEM

NATURE OF THE SYSTEM

1. Its origin and growth. The strict formalism of the *legis actiones* procedure (*see* XXI), involving the possibility of losing an action because of incorrectly-recited formulae, became a hindrance to the development of effective legal procedure. During the earlier Republic there grew up the practice of a plaintiff's requesting an action from the Praetor and, in certain cases, defendant's requesting an *exceptio* (*see* **23** below). Flexible procedural formulae became available in which were contained precise terms of reference to the judge and a definition of the questions he was to decide.

Lex Aebutia (*see* XXI, **4**) allowed the use of this type of formula in actions between Roman citizens, and Augustus, by *Leges Juliae Judiciorum Privatorum* (17 B.C.) allowed the formulary procedure to be used in all types of claim. During the classical period it was the basis of civil procedure.

2. Its advantages.

(a) No formal acts or style of oral procedure were required from the parties to proceedings *in jure*.

(b) Formulae were capable of adaptation to any claim considered by the Praetor to be equitable.

TYPES OF ACTION UNDER THE FORMULARY SYSTEM

3. Civil and Praetorian. Civil actions were created by *lex*, or based on the civil law; praetorian actions were formulated by the Praetor on the basis of civil law actions adapted to meet new cases.

4. In rem and In personam. Actions *in rem* were based on the assertion of a right "against the world"; actions *in personam* on the assertion of a right against a person.

5. Temporal and Perpetual. Temporal actions had to be brought within a defined period of time; perpetual actions had no time limit.

6. Directa and Utilis. The former were actions created under the civil law; the latter were adapted from civil law actions by the Praetor.

7. Popularis and Privata. The former allowed any member of the public to sue for a penalty (*see*, for example, XX, 2); the latter allowed only the injured party to sue.

8. Stricti Juris and Bona Fidei. This was a very important classification. In the former actions no equitable defences (*see* **23** below) were admitted unless specifically pleaded by defendant; in the latter actions the *judex* was allowed to take equitable defences into account even if they had not been pleaded specifically.

9. In Jus Concepta and In Factum Concepta. The former were based on civil law rights; the latter asserted rights created by the Praetor.

EVENTS PRECEDING THE TRIAL

10. The Summons. This remained, as in *legis actio* procedure (*see* XXI, 5), a private matter for the plaintiff based on the XII Tables. Certain modifications were made by the Praetors:

(a) *It became an offence* for a person summoned to refuse to obey.

(b) *It became an offence to rescue*, or to help the escape of a person summoned.

(c) *Certain people could not be summoned*, *e.g.* a priest in the act of worship, a *judex* participating in a trial, a magistrate possessing *imperium* (full authority), a complainant's ascendants or his patron (without the Praetor's permission), a man who was inside his own house at the time the summons was made.

THE TRIAL

11. General. As in the *legis actio* procedure, the formulary procedure involved two stages: *in jure* and *in judicio*.

12. In Jure.

(a) *The plaintiff, in defendant's presence, outlined his claim* and asked the magistrate for a particular action. Where the claim could not be met by an action outlined in the Praetor's Edict his request was not granted, but, where possible, an *actio in factum* (*see* **9** above) could then be requested. Where plaintiff's claim was considered unworthy of litigation it was rejected.

(b) *The magistrate had to consider at this stage certain matters, e.g.:*

   (i) Was the plaintiff's claim within the scope of formulary procedure?
   (ii) Had the parties capacity to sue and be sued?
   (iii) Had the parties capacity to plead before the court?

13. The defendant's role in jure.

(a) *He might admit the claim* (*confessio in jure*). Such an admission formed a basis for subsequent execution of the claim.

(b) *He might deny plaintiff's facts, or his rights* in the matter. Such a denial was construed as willingness to defend the action.

(c) *He might accept plaintiff's statement of rights and facts,* but might assert other matters which barred the action. In such a case an *exceptio* (*see* **23** below) could be inserted in the formula, with the magistrate's agreement. Plaintiff could request, in such a case, a *replicatio*, as a reply to defendant's request (*see* note to **23** below).

(d) *He might neither accept nor deny plaintiff's claim* nor ask for an *exceptio*. In such a case, if the action was *in rem* he was not obliged to defend. But by a further *actio ad exhibendum*, or, in the case of land, the *interdictum quem fundum*, he could be obliged to appear as defendant, unless he wished to be deprived of the *res* without legal argument as to its ownership. If the action was *in personam* he was regarded as *indefensus* (one who did not defend himself). By order of the Praetor execution could be levied against the property of an *indefensus*.

14. Choosing the judge. The next stage, after an indication by the magistrate that he was willing to grant an action, was the choice of either a single judge (*judex unus*) or a group of judges.

(a) *The judex unus was a free male person* aged 25 or over, whose name was inscribed on an official list (*album judicum selectorum*). Plaintiff and defendant had to agree on a choice, but a continued refusal of names by defendant rendered him *indefensus* (*see* **13**(d) above).
(b) *Groups or boards of judges* (*recuperatores*) might sit in serious cases involving public issues, *e.g.* the liberty of a person.

15. Judicium dari. After the type of action had been agreed and a judge had been nominated, the formula was drafted (*see* **18–21** below). The magistrate issued an order for the trial and issue was now joined between the parties.

16. Litis contestatio. The stage reached in **15** above was known as *litis contestatio* (joinder of issue). After that moment it was not possible to alter the pleadings. The effects of *litis contestatio* were:

(a) *Parties were henceforth obliged to accept* the judgment.
(b) *Plaintiff could not bring another action* on the same subject matter.
(c) *The property which was the subject of the action* could not be alienated until the action had been decided.
(d) *Any period of limitation* imposed on the right of action was interrupted.
See also XV, **14**.

17. In Judicio.

(a) *The judge's terms of references* were based strictly on the formula.
(b) *He was obliged to hear evidence from both parties.*
(c) *His judgment* (*sententia*) *was pronounced in the presence* of both parties and was in terms of money. A judge who was unable to reach a decision had to take an oath that the matter was not clear to him (*rem sibi non liquere*), upon which he was discharged and replaced by another judge. A majority decision was effective in the case of a group of

judges; an equally-divided vote was construed in defendant's favour.

NOTE
(i) *Execution of the judgment* did not follow immediately upon the judgment, but required further proceedings (*see* **24–25** below).
(ii) *The judex could consult advisers (adsessores).*
(iii) *Parties could be represented in litigation by a cognitor or procurator.* The *cognitor* was named at proceedings in *jure* and was thus authorised by the court. The *procurator* was not authorised in this manner; he had to give security that he would meet any obligations imposed by the judgment.
(iv) *Tutors and curators (see* VII) could also act as procedural representatives.
(v) *The parties' case was often placed in the hands of advocates.* Deaf persons, and persons under 17, were prohibited from pleading their own case. An advocate was provided by the Praetor if such persons had not one of their own. Under the Empire advocates were known as *advocati* or *causadici*; prior to that they were known as *patroni*. An advocate might be assisted by another lawyer known as a *monitor*.
(vi) *A plaintiff who had brought a claim which he knew was unjust* could be condemned in a subsequent action for *calumnia* (= false accusation) to a penalty of one-tenth of his original claim.

THE FORMULA

18. Its contents. The formula was drawn up during proceedings *in jure*. It included the nomination of a judge, a statement of the issue to be tried, and a direction to the judge to condemn or absolve the defendant. The clauses of the formula were governed in their content by fixed rules and were usually set out in a formal order.

19. Order of the clauses. Clauses were generally arranged in the following pattern:

20. The clauses.

(a) *Nominatio.* Nomination of the judge.
(b) *Demonstratio.* Statement of the facts upon which the claim was based.
(c) *Intentio.* Statement of the question to be considered by the judge.
(d) *Adjudicatio.* Direction to the judge to adjudicate shares. Used only in partition actions (*see* **21**, note (i) below).
(e) *Condemnatio.* Direction to the judge to condemn or absolve the defendant.

> NOTE: *Praescriptio* and *Exceptio* are considered in **22–23** below.

21. Examples of the Formula.

(a) [*Nominatio*] "Let Titius be judge: [*Demonstratio*] whereas X sold the slave Y to Z: [*Intentio*] whatever Z ought to pay X on that account in good faith: [*Condemnatio*] Judge, condemn Z to pay to X. If it does not so appear, absolve him." (An action of sale brought by X, the vendor.)
(b) [*Nominatio*] "Let Titius be judge: [*Demonstratio*] inasmuch as A has deposited with B the bronze ornament which is in question: [*Intentio*] whatsoever, in respect thereof B should give to or do for A in good faith: [*Condemnatio*] Judge, condemn B to A. If it does not appear, absolve him". (An action in the case of deposit brought by the depositor, A (*see* XVI, **13**).)

> NOTE
>
> (i) Not all the clauses enumerated in **20** above appeared in all formulae. Thus, *adjudicatio* (*e.g.* "As much as ought to be adjudged, judge, adjudge to X or Y") appeared only in *actiones communi dividundo*, between partners, or between neighbours to determine boundaries (*finium regundorum*). In cases of *praejudicia* (which involved the answering of a preliminary question of fact), the entire formula might be: "Let Titius be judge as to whether X is free or a slave."
>
> (ii) The *condemnatio* clause usually called for the payment of a sum of money. Where the *judex* was instructed to condemn in a stated sum, the *condemnatio* was said to be *certa*; where the judge could use his discretion, the *condemnatio* was said to be *incerta*; where the judge could use his discretion, but not so as to exceed a

stated sum, it was said to be *condemnatio incerta cum taxatione*.

22. Praescriptio. (*Prae scribere* = to write before). It was possible to insert, before the *demonstratio*, a clause which limited the scope of the action.

EXAMPLE: Brutus has to pay Publius a certain sum of money each week for a year. Brutus fails to pay and Publius sues him for the outstanding instalments, but he does not wish the action to prejudice his right to sue for future unpaid instalments (*see* **16**(b) above). Publius was allowed to insert a *praescriptio pro actore* before the *demonstratio*, e.g. "*Ea res agatur cujus rei dies fuit.*" ("Let the action be confined to claims which have accrued.")

23. Exceptio.

(a) The *exceptio* was introduced by the Praetor and was inserted in the formula before the *condemnatio*. It consisted of a negative clause alleging facts which, if established by defendant, would defeat plaintiff's claim.

(b) *A dilatory exception* asserted that the action was premature, e.g. the *exceptio pacti conventi*, under which it could be asserted that A had agreed not to sue B for a stated period of time. *A peremptory exception* raised a defence, which, on equitable grounds, might defeat the plaintiff, e.g. where X was suing Y on a contract induced by the intimidation of Y.

(c) Examples of *exceptiones* were: *exceptio metus* (intimidation); *exceptio doli* ("*Si in ea re nihil dolo malo A factum sit neque fiat. . . .*") ("If in this matter A has not acted or is not acting in a fraudulent manner. . . ."); *exceptio pacti de non petendo* (agreement not to sue) ("*Si inter Aulum et Numerium non convenit ne ea pecunia peteretur. . . .*") ("If Aulus and Numerius did not agree that the money should not be claimed. . . .")

NOTE: An *exceptio* could be met with a *replicatio*; thus, where defendant pleads as an *exceptio* an agreement not to sue, plaintiff may enter a *replicatio* (replication) pleading a further agreement to allow him to sue.

EVENTS FOLLOWING THE TRIAL

24. Execution on the person. *Legis actio per manus injectionem* (*see* XXI, **10**) gave way to the *actio judicati* (action on the judgment). Where the defendant who had been condemned wished to question the judgment (*e.g.* as to whether the judgment was authorised by the formula) he could enter a defence, but if he failed he and his surety (necessary to this action) were liable in twice the amount of the judgment. Where no defence to the *actio judicati* was entered, defendant passed into the plaintiff's bondage, where he remained until the debt was satisfied.

25. Execution on the property. The procedure adopted originated under the Praetor Publius Rutilius (*c.* 118 B.C.). For details, *see* XV, **19–21**.

NOTE ON LEGAL PRECEDENT: There was no systematised form of reference to legal precedent in Roman Law. A judge was not generally bound by previous decisions. But Imperial Rescripts (*see* II, **20**) were binding (*see* also II, **19**(c) and (d)). One of Justinian's Constitutions states, ". . . we decree that every interpretation of statutes rendered by the Emperor, whatever in respect of petitions or of causes in action or in whatever other manner pronounced, shall be of indisputable authority." In another Constitution he states, "No judge or arbitrator is to deem himself bound by juristic opinions which he considers erroneous: still less by the decision of learned prefects or other judgments. If an erroneous decision has been given, it should not be allowed to spread and so to corrupt the judgment of other magistrates. Decisions should be based on laws, not on precedents."

PROGRESS TEST 22

1. How was the introduction of the formulary system brought about? (**1**)

2. What were the main advantages of the formulary system? (**2**)

3. Distinguish (a) civil and praetorian actions, (b) *actiones stricti juris* and *bonae fidei*. (**3, 8**)

4. What modifications were made by the Praetors in the summons under the formulary system? (**10**)

5. Outline the defendant's role *in jure* under the formulary system. **(13)**

6. Explain (a) *judicium dari*, (b) *judex unus*. **(14, 15)**

7. Define *litis contestatio*. What was its significance? **(16)**

8. Enumerate the clauses in a formula. **(20)**

9. What was the usual order of the clauses in a formula? **(19)**

10. Distinguish the clauses in the following formula:
"Let Seius be judge. Whereas Gaius sold a golden casket to Flavius, whatever Flavius ought to pay Gaius on that account in good faith, Judge, condemn him to pay to Gaius. If it does not so appear, then absolve him." **(20, 21)**

11. What was an *exceptio*? **(23)**

12. "The introduction of the *exceptio* by the Praetor was of major importance in the development of Roman Law." Discuss. **(23)**

13. How did execution on the person follow an action under the formulary system? **(24)**

CHAPTER XXIII

EXTRAORDINARY PROCEDURE: PRAETORIAN INTERDICTS AND OTHER REMEDIES: APPEALS

COGNITIO EXTRAORDINARIA

1. Decline of the Formulary System. In the later years of the Principate the formulary system declined. The bipartite form of the hearings (*in jure* and *in judicio*) disappeared and, with it, the procedures and styles appropriate to the formulary system. In A.D. 342 Constantine prohibited the use of *juris formulae*.

2. Nature of Cognitio Extraordinaria. Some trials, heard by the Praetor himself, because of their particular nature (*e.g. fideicommissa—see* XIII, 32) were known as *cognitiones* and were considered outside the ordinary kind of suit (*extra ordinem*). In time the procedure adopted in this kind of hearing became common. Under the procedure *extra ordinem* the entire hearing up to the judgment took place before the magistrate; reference of the case to a *judex* disappeared.

EVENTS PRECEDING THE TRIAL

3. The Summons (evocatio). A written summons was served by plaintiff acting under official authority (*denuntiatio ex auctoritate*) or by an officer of the court at defendant's house. Defendant's failure to appear in court could result in procedure by default against him.

4. Libellus Conventionis. From *c.* A.D. 400 proceedings commenced with a submission by plaintiff of his statement of claim (*libellus conventionis*) to the magistrate. The *libellus* included not only the claim, but its basis in law. Formulae (as in the formulary system) were not used. The *libellus* was

196

examined by the magistrate and then served on defendant, who was expected to submit his reply (*libellus contradictionis*) within twenty days.

Plaintiff and defendant were obliged to give security for their attendance at court. A defendant who refused to give security (*cautio: judicio sistendi*) was imprisoned until the hearings had ended. A defendant who refused to defend an *actio in rem* was deprived of the *res* (the subject matter of the action) which was then given to plaintiff.

THE TRIAL

5. Pleadings. Parties stated their case (the plaintiff by *narratio*; the defendant by *contradictio*), after they and their advocates had taken an oath (*jusjurandum calumniae*). These pleadings were recorded by a court official and the exact nature of the dispute was decided.

6. Litis contestatio. This title (used for a different stage in proceedings under the formulary system, *see* XXII, **16**) was given to the commencement of the trial after initial pleadings.

7. The Defence. Peremptory exceptions (*see* XXII, **23**(b)) could be pleaded. Defendant could make an admission before the court (*confessio in jure*) which led to judgment immediately.

8. Evidence. Witnesses could be summoned officially and were generally compelled to give evidence. Documents drafted by professional scribes (*instrumenta publice confecta*) were considered to provide weightier evidence than mere oral testimony. Justinian gave the same evidential weight to documents attested by three or more witnesses (*instrumenta quasi publice confecta*).

9. The Judgment. The judgment was put into written form and was read out in public. Specific performance could be directed. A judgment was not required to be in money terms (*compare* XXII, **17**(c)). The unsuccessful party was directed to pay costs.

EVENTS FOLLOWING THE TRIAL

10. Execution of the judgment. Under Justinian judgment had to be satisfied within four months. Execution on the person, resulting in imprisonment, still existed. Execution of a judgment for a sum of money was levied against the debtor's property by *pignus ex judicati causa captum*. The estate of an insolvent debtor was liquidated by *bonorum distractio* (*see* XV, **21**). An order for specific performance would be enforced by officials of the court.

PRAETORIAN INTERDICTS AND OTHER REMEDIES

11. The nature of Praetorian Interdicts. An interdict (*interdicere* = to prohibit) took the form of an order, issued by the Praetor, requiring a person to do or not to do some thing. It was issued after a plaintiff had petitioned the Praetor. If the interdict was ignored or contravened, the plaintiff's petition became the basis of a trial by a *judex privatus*, or *recuperatores* (*see* XXII, **14**(b)).

12. Classification of Interdicts. There were several classifications:

(a) *Restitutory* (an order to restore or transfer); *Prohibitory* (an order forbidding some thing); *Exhibitory* (an order to produce some thing).
(b) *Possessory* (requiring something to be acquired—*adipiscendae*, retained—*retinendae*, regained—*reciperandae possessionis causa comparata*); *Non-possessory* (ordering something to be done or not done).
(c) *Single* (when the applicant for an interdict was plaintiff in subsequent proceedings); *Double* (when each party was alternately plaintiff and defendant (*see: uti possidetis* below)).

UTI POSSIDETIS AND UTRUBI

13. Their meaning. *Uti possidetis* was a Praetorian interdict used for deciding rights of possession in immovables. *Utrubi* was an interdict used for deciding rights of possession in movables. They were prohibitory and double interdicts (*interdicta duplicia*). The issuing of these interdicts prohibited both parties from using force to interfere with existing possession.

NOTE: These interdicts supported only such possession as was *nec vi, nec clam, nec precario, i.e.* obtained from the adversary neither by force, by stealth, nor with his permission.

14. Procedure in uti possidetis.

(a) *Following the issuing of the interdict* the parties fictitiously ejected each other (*vis ex conventu*).

(b) *Each summoned the other* and alleged a contravention of the interdict.

(c) *Interim possession was put up to auction* between the parties (*fructuus licitatio*); the highest bidder stipulated for a penal sum (*fructuaria stipulatio*), or gave security for satisfaction of the judgment (*satisdatio judicatum solvi*).

(d) *Both parties* (*as plaintiffs and defendants*) *wagered penal sums* and entered into a *sponsio* and *restipulatio*, whereby each would give or receive penal sums, depending on the judgment.

(e) *The four actions* (based on double *sponsiones* and *restipulationes*) were heard by a judge.

(f) *A decision in favour of the interim possessor* resulted in condemnation of the other party in the sum of the two penal wagers.

(g) *A decision against the interim possessor* resulted in his condemnation in the two wagers, and a further action for the recovery of interim profits, or on the *fructuaria stipulatio*.

(h) *A further action, judicium secutorium,* was brought against an unsuccessful party who failed to deliver up possession.

UNDE VI AND QUORUM BONORUM

15. Unde Vi. An interdict *unde vi* was a restitutory order granted to a person who wished to recover land from which he had been ejected by force. The interdict had two forms:

(a) *de vi armata*, used in a case of armed force;

(b) *quotidianum quotidiana*, used where ordinary force had been employed.

16. Quorum Bonorum. The interdict *quorum bonorum* was a remedy sought by a successor to whom *bonorum possessio* had been given by the Praetor (*see* XIII, **33**) and whose title was disputed. It was also available to a person who had indicated, by some act, his intention to claim as *bonorum possessor*, and against a person who claimed as successor or who had seized without title.

OTHER PRAETORIAN REMEDIES

17. Restitutio in integrum (restoration to the original position). This remedy was available, on grounds of equity, for the reinstatement of a person in the legal position he had occupied prior to a particular event. It was granted only where no relief was available by operation of the ordinary law, where the person had suffered some prejudice from the operation of the law, and where both parties could be reinstated in their previous positions. Application had to be made within one year, extended to four years by Justinian. The applicant had to show certain grounds (*justa causa*) for his claim, *e.g.* fraud, intimidation, change of status, minority, excusable mistake.

18. Missio in possessionem (putting in possession). Under certain circumstances the Praetor might place one person in possession of another's property, as in the case of an insolvent debtor (*see* XV, **19**).

APPEALS

19. During the Republic. There was no right of appeal in civil actions during the Republic. The intercession (*intercessio*) of magistrates of equal or higher standing acted as a veto on a judgment, and it was possible for a private individual to make a formal demand (*appellatio*) for the exercise of such a veto.

20. During the Empire. A regular system of appeals was set up. An appeal from magistrates in Rome went to the Prefect of the City, thence to the Praetorian Prefect, or, in certain cases, to the Emperor himself. Appeals from municipal magistrates in Italy and the provinces went to the Governors of the provinces, then to the Praetorian Prefect. Under Constantine an appeal was allowed from the *judex* to the magistrate who had appointed him. Under Justinian the imperial court (*auditorium principis*) would not entertain any appeal based on subject matter less than the value of twenty pounds of gold;

cases involving a lower value went to a judge, whose decision was final.

21. Appeal Procedure.

(a) Notice of appeal could be given orally, on hearing the judgment, but where this was not done written notice might be given (under Justinian) within ten days.
(b) An appellant who presented a written petition (*libellus appellatorius*) had to state the names of the appellant and respondent, the judgment in issue, and the grounds of appeal.
(c) The judge forwarded the petition to the court of Appeal. A judge who refused, without good reason, to forward an appeal, could be fined.
(d) All documents had to be sent to the court of Appeal within twenty (later, thirty) days.
(e) New evidence was admissible in the court of Appeal.

> NOTE
> (i) There was no appeal from the execution of a judgment unless the official who had carried it out had exceeded his authority.
> (ii) Vexatious appeals were disallowed.
> (iii) Parties, their agents and sureties could appeal.

PROGRESS TEST 23

1. What was the nature of the *cognitio extraordinaria* system? (2)
2. Explain the nature of the *libellus conventionis*. (4)
3. Outline the events following a trial under the *cognitio extraordinaria* system. (10)
4. Illustrate the significance of the Praetorian interdict. (11)
5. Distinguish (a) restitutory and prohibitory interdicts, (b) single and double interdicts. (12)
6. Give an account of the procedure following the issue of an interdict *uti possidetis*. (14)
7. What was the interdict *unde vi*? (15)
8. Under what circumstances would the Praetor allow the remedy of *restitutio in integrum*? (17)
9. Outline the system of appeals during the Empire. (20)
10. Explain (a) *intercessio*, (b) *libellus appellatorius*. (19, 21)

APPENDIX I

DATES IN THE HISTORY OF ROMAN LAW

B.C.	
753	Foundation of Rome
510	Expulsion of the Kings
451–448 *c.*	The XII Tables
367	Office of *Praetor* and *Curule Aediles* instituted
304	*Jus Flavianum* published
300	*Lex Ogulnia*
287	*Lex Hortensia*
286	*Lex Aquilia*
242	Appointment of *Praetor Peregrinus*
200	*Lex Plaetoria*
120 *c.*	*Lex Aebutia*
91–89	The Social War
49	Julius Caesar attains power
44	Julius Caesar assassinated
40	*Lex Falcidia*
27–14 A.D.	The Principate of Augustus
	Jus Respondendi instituted
	Fideicommissa and *Codicilli introduced*

A.D.	
4	*Lex Aelia Sentia*
9	*Lex Julia et Papia Poppaea*
14–37	Tiberius
37–41	Caligula
41–54	Claudius
69 *c.*	Sc. Macedonianum
54–68	Nero
69–79	Vespasian
79–81	Titus
81–96	Domitian
96–98	Nerva
98–117	Trajan
117–138	Hadrian
	Edictum Perpetuum of Salvius Julianus

202

138–161	Antoninus Pius
	Institutes of Gaius
161–169	M. Aurelius and L. Verus
169–180	M. Aurelius
180–193	Commodus
193–211	Septimius Severus
211–217	Caracalla
222–235	Alexander Severus
238–244	Gordian
285–286	Diocletian
286–305	Diocletian and Maximian
	Division of the Empire
305–306	Constantius I and Galerius
306	Constantius I, Galerius and Constantine
306	*Codex Gregorianus*
307–311	Galerius, Constantine and Licinius
311–323	Constantine and Licinius
323–337	Constantine
364	Valentinian II and Valens
365 *c.*	*Codex Hermogenianus*
408–450	Theodosius I, Emperor of the Eastern Empire
425–455	Valentinian III, Emperor of the Western Empire
426	Law of Citations
438 *c.*	*Codex Theodosianus*
457–474	Leo II, Emperor of the Eastern Empire
476	End of the Western Empire
474–491	Zeno, Emperor of the East
491–518	Anastasius I
500 *c.*	*Edictum Theodorici*
506	*Breviarium Alaricianum*
517 *c.*	*Lex Romanum Burgundionum*
518–527	Justin
527–565	Justinian
529	*Codex Vetus*
529–532	*Quinquaginta Decisiones*
533	Publication of Digest and Institutes
534	*Codex Repetitae Praelectionis*

EXAMINATION TECHNIQUE

1. The general purpose of law examinations. Examinations in legal subjects are designed to test the student's knowledge and comprehension of legal principles, together with his ability to apply those principles with precision in the solution of problems. The successful candidate in an examination on Roman Law will have demonstrated a thorough knowledge of basic principles and an ability to make use of those principles in a sustained and logical argument.

2. Types of question. Questions on Roman Law tend to be of three main types:

(a) *Those demanding a purely factual answer, e.g.*

    (i) Define *usufruct.* By what methods could it be created?
    (ii) Compare and contrast *tutela impuberum* with *tutela perpetua mulierum.*

(b) *Those calling for a discussion, e.g.*

    (i) "Essentially the Roman slave had no rights." Discuss.
    (ii) Evaluate and discuss the main contribution of Justinian to Roman Law.

(c) *Those requiring the solution of a problem, e.g.*

    (i) Aulus buys a helmet from Balbus, not knowing that it has been stolen from Cassius. Cassius sees Aulus wearing the helmet and asks for its return. Aulus refuses and Cassius takes it by force. Advise Aulus.
    (ii) Sempronius meets Maevius, slave of Brutus, in a crowded street. Sempronius strikes Maevius in the face, shouting, "Thus I show my contempt for your worthless master!" Maevius is blinded in one eye as a result. Advise Brutus.

3. The Factual Question. The answer to this type of question should be characterised by precision, relevance and logical sequence. Thus, in 2(a)(i) above, a clear definition is required, followed by a precise account of the ways in which a usufruct could be created. The greater the number of well-marshalled and relevant facts, the higher will be the mark awarded to the student.

4. The Discussion Question. This kind of question demands an answer based on a solid foundation of fact. The discussion must arise out of the facts. It should be interesting and informative and, above all, relevant. The question at 2(b)(i) above demands, first, an exposition of the general status of the Roman slave. How did this status affect his position under the law? Had he any rights? If so, what were they? What was their real worth? Avoid digressions into the social position of the slave, unless they illustrate a particular point in law. Do not hesitate to give your own point of view, always provided that you can support it by factual argument.

5. The Problem Question. This type of question occupies an important place in examinations on Roman Law. It tests a student's knowledge of principles and his power to apply them. The technique required for a good answer should be based on the following method:

(a) Read the question carefully.

(b) Place the problem in its historical context. Does the problem refer to the law as it stood, say, during the classical era? Does it state, or assume, conditions in the Republic, or under Justinian?

(c) Identify the precise principles involved. Thus 2(c)(ii) above involves the principles of delict in general, and of *injuria, damnum injuria datum, Lex Aquilia,* etc.

(d) Apply the principles to the facts of the problem.

(e) Give your solution to the problem on the basis of (d).

6. In the examination room. You should have arrived for your examination having revised extensively. In planning your pre-examination revision allow time for the practice of questions from previous examination papers. The following points are suggested as being of particular importance in the actual examination:

(a) *Follow the instructions carefully.* Where questions have to be selected from particular sections of the paper, this instruction must not be ignored.

(b) *Answer the exact number of questions required.* You will gain no extra marks by answering additional questions; you will lose marks, of course, by answering too few questions.

(c) *Plan your time.* Do not leave yourself with only a few minutes in which to answer the final question.

(d) *Plan each answer methodically.* Do not begin to write your answer until you have made a rough sketch of its contents. Select facts, recognise principles and plan your answer so that it illustrates a rational sequence of thought. Lucidity and objectivity characterised much of the writings of the great jurists. Let these qualities be the basis of your examination work!

7. Illustration of question and answer.

Question. *"Olim itaque tribus modis in manum conveniabant."* ("In early times women used to pass into *manus* in three ways.") Explain this statement by Gaius.

Answer: In early times the very extensive powers exerted by the *paterfamilias* over all the members of his household were known as *manus*. Later the term came to be applied solely to the power of the *paterfamilias* over the wife of the house. The wife (*uxor in manu*) was in the position of a daughter to her husband; her property was his and her rights of succession were the same as those of her children.

Manus marriage came about in three ways: first, by *confarreatio*, secondly, by *coemptio*, and, thirdly, by *usus*.

Confarreatio involved a religious ceremony which was available only to members of the patrician class. Ten witnesses had to be present at a ceremonial rite in which a wheaten cake (*farreus panis*) was sacrificed by the bride in honour of Jupiter. As a result of the ceremony the bride passed into the *manus* of her husband.

Coemptio involved a fictitious sale of the bride by the process of *mancipatio*, and was based on the acquiring of ownership by *mancipatio*. Five witnesses and a *libripens* (balance holder) were required. The bride was bought for an *as* by the person into whose *manus* she passed after his recital of the traditional formula, *"Hanc ego mulierem meam esse aio."* ("I declare this woman to be mine.")

By *usus* a woman passed into the *manus* of her husband after cohabitation for one year. No particular ceremony was required. By the law of the XII Tables a woman could prevent herself passing into *manus* by absenting herself from the husband for three nights (*trinoctium*) in the year.

As Roman society changed so did the importance attached to *manus*. In the early Empire it was enacted that *manus* could not be brought about by *confarreatio*. Before the time of Justinian *confarreatio* and *coemptio* had become obsolete, while *nsus* had been abolished under the Republic.

SPECIMEN TEST PAPERS

PAPER I

Answer any *five* questions. Time: Three hours.

1. What is meant by the classical period of Roman Law? What were the chief sources of law in this period?

[*Intermediate Laws, Sept.* 1965]

2. Describe the main features of the Roman law of divorce.

[*Intermediate Laws, Sept.* 1965]

3. Distinguish between
(a) *locatio conductio rei* and *emphyteusis*; and
(b) *locatio conductio operis* and *locatio conductio operarum*.

[*Intermediate Laws, Sept.* 1963]

4. Consider the importance of *testamenti factio* in the Roman law of wills.

5. A alleges that he deposited a collection of old coins with B for safe keeping, and that B has sold the coins and kept the proceeds. Draft the appropriate formula for an action by A in A.D. 100 on the assumptions (a) that A agreed to pay B 5 *aurei* a month for his trouble, and, alternatively (b) that no payment was agreed upon. [*Intermediate Laws, June* 1965]

6. (a) Distinguish, with examples, between a pact and an innominate contract.
(b) X offers to lend Y his chariot for a week-end drive in the country if Y will dig over X's garden for him. Y digs the garden, but X then refuses to lend him the chariot. Advise Y.

[*Intermediate Laws, June* 1964]

7. Advise A in the following cases:
(a) A buys a slave from B. At the time of the sale B informs A that the slave is "intelligent but very highly strung." He does not disclose the fact that six months previously the slave had a nervous breakdown. Nine months later the slave has another breakdown, and A incurs considerable expense in having him treated.
(b) In A.D. 550, B tricks A into signing a document "as witness" by falsely pretending that the document concerns a transaction between B and C. In fact, it reads "I, the undersigned, promise to pay B on demand 100 *aurei*" and bears

no signature except A's. Two years later B demands the 100 *aurei* from A. [*Intermediate Laws, June* 1963]

8. Explain the following distinctions and state their importance:

(a) rustic and urban servitudes;

(b) *stricti juris* and *bonae fidei* actions;

(c) *res mobiles* and *immobiles*. [*Intermediate Laws, Sept.* 1962]

9. As a practical joke, A puts a drug into B's wine at a dinner knowing that B is going to drive home. On the way home B succumbs to the effect of the drug, falls asleep at the reins, and crashes. B's nose is broken, his horse is killed, and his chariot wrecked. D, who is hit by the chariot, loses a leg. Discuss.

[*Intermediate Laws, Sept.* 1962]

PAPER II

Answer any *five* questions. Time: Three hours.

1. Distinguish between *jus civile*, *jus gentium* and *jus honorarium*. [*Intermediate Laws, June* 1965]

2. "The laws of The Roman people consist of leges, plebiscites, senatusconsults, imperial constitutions, edicts of those possessing the right to issue them, and answers of the learned." (Gaius, I.2). To what extent was this statement true when Gaius was writing?

[*Intermediate Laws, Sept.* 1963]

3. "Marriage in Roman Law is an institution of social fact." Explain this statement, and distinguish between free marriage and *manus* marriage. [*Intermediate Laws, June* 1964]

4. What were the main features of the formulary system of procedure? Why is it important in the history of Roman Law?

[*Intermediate Laws, Sept.* 1964]

5. Outline the law of intestate succession (a) under the XII Tables, (b) under Justinian.

6. Distinguish between the following and discuss their importance:

(a) *heres necessarius* and *heres extraneus* and

(b) *legatum per vindicationem* and *legatum sinendi modi*.

7. E bought and paid for a horse and a leather saddle in a market. Six months later he was told that the horse had been stolen from F a year before. Eighteen months after the purchase F appeared at E's farm with a group of armed men and took away the horse and saddle. E was wounded in the disorder which occurred. Advise E. [*Intermediate Laws, Sept.* 1963]

8. (a) Compare the legal position of the slave with that of the son in power in classical law.

(b) A, who resides in Rome, appoints his slave, B, as manager of his fruit farm in Sicily. At the end of the season B sells the fruit crop at a handsome profit. B now orders new equipment for the farm from C, buys an amphora of wine from D for his own use, and gambles away most of the money. Advise C and D, who remain unpaid. *[Intermediate Laws, June* 1965]

9. What role does the use of written documents play in the formation of contracts in Roman Law?

Was there truly a literal contract in the law of Justinian?
[Intermediate Laws, Sept. 1961]

PAPER III

Answer any *five* questions. Time: Three hours.

1. "With the coming of imperial times there came also profound changes in the ways in which Roman Law was made." Discuss.
[Intermediate Laws, Sept. 1961]

2. (a) What is *manus* marriage, and what are its effects?

(b) Describe the reforms made by Justinian in the law relating to *adoptio*. *[Intermediate Laws, Sept.* 1962]

3. Discuss (a) how far a slave was protected from his master's harshness, and (b) how far the master's legal position could be affected by his slave's conduct: (i) in A.D. 100; (ii) in A.D. 530.
[Intermediate Laws, Sept. 1961]

4. Consider the importance of (a) the interdict, and (b) the *exceptio* in the development of Roman Law.
[Intermediate Laws, June 1964]

5. "The formula tells the *judex* all he needs to know about the issue in the case." Explain this statement. Do you agree?
[Intermediate Laws, Sept. 1963]

6. R borrows a toga from S to go to a dinner given by T. Late in the evening, when R is lying in a drunken stupor before the house, another guest for a joke empties a chamber-pot out of the window and drenches R. Next day, R takes the toga to P, a cleaner, and agrees to pay 100 *sesterces* for it to be cleaned. During the night it is stolen by Q, who is seen running off with it by one of P's slaves, but when he is finally caught Q no longer has the toga. Discuss. *[Intermediate Laws, Sept.* 1961]

7. (a) Discuss the rules concerning disherison.

(b) What changes were made by Justinian to the *querela inofficiosi testamenti*?

8. (a) A agrees to buy a slave from B "when my brother comes to Rome" at a price to be fixed by C. A's brother arrives in Rome,

and B hands over the slave to A, although C has not yet in fact fixed the price. Soon afterwards, it turns out that the slave is suffering from leprosy, and two of A's other slaves become infected with the disease. Advise A.

(b) What common characteristics do the four real contracts have? [*Intermediate Laws, June* 1964]

9. L agreed to buy all the apples produced at the next harvest from M's orchard, on condition that M provided transport to the market. M loaded the apples on to his cart when they had been gathered in, and set off for the market. On the way, however, he was involved in a collision with a chariot driven negligently by R. Many of the apples were spoilt, and M was injured. A passer-by, S, paid 50 *solidi* to T, a doctor, for treatment for the unconscious M, but owing to T's incorrect diagnosis the treatment was ineffective and M died.

Advise M's heir as to any claims and liabilities he may have.
[*Intermediate Laws, Sept.* 1963]

INDEX

213